DISCARD

THE ILLUSTRATED HISTORY OF THE WORLD

1
The Earliest Civilizations

2
Rome and the Ancient World

3
The Dark Ages

4
The Middle Ages

5
The Age of Discovery
(1500–1650)

6
Conflict and Change
(1650–1800)

7
The Nineteenth Century

8
The Modern World

The Nineteenth Century

PREFACE

The Illustrated History of the World is a unique series of eight volumes covering the entire scope of human history, from the days of the nomadic hunters up to the present. Each volume surveys significant events and personages, key political and economic developments, and the critical forces that inspired change, in both institutions and the everyday life of people around the globe.

The books are organized on a spread-by-spread basis, allowing ease of access and depth of coverage on a wide range of fascinating topics and time periods within any one volume. Each spread serves as a kind of mini-essay, in words and pictures, of its subject. The text—cogent, concise and lively—is supplemented by an impressive array of illustrations (original art, full-color photographs, maps, diagrams) and features (glossary, index, time charts, further reading listings). Taking into account the new emphasis on multicultural education, special care has been given to presenting a balanced portrait of world history: the volumes in the series explore all civilizations— whether it's the Mayans in Mexico, the Shoguns in Japan or the Sumerians in the Middle East.

The Nineteenth Century

Michael Pollard

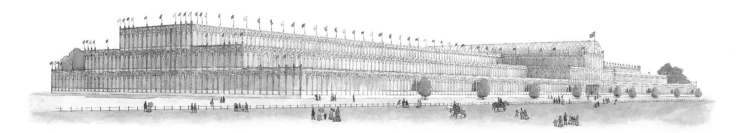

Facts On File

Facts On File, Inc.
460 Park Avenue South
New York NY 10016

Library of Congress Cataloging-in-Publication Data

Pollard, Michael, 1931–
The nineteenth century/Michael Pollard.
p.   cm — (The Illustrated history of the world)
Includes bibliographical references and index.
Summary: A history of the world during the nineteenth century.
Includes the early Industrial Revolution in Europe, growing colonial
empires, conflicts over slavery, and America's emergence as an
industrial giant.
ISBN 0-8160-2791-9
1. History, Modern—19th century—Juvenile literature.
[1. History, Modern—19th century.] I. Title. II. Series.
D358.P65 1993
909.81—dc20
92-19080
CIP
AC

ISBN 0 8160 2791 9

Facts On File books are available at special discounts when purchased
in bulk quantities for businesses, associations, institutions or sales
promotions. Please call our Special Sales Department in New York at
212/683-2244 (dial 800/322-8755 except in NY, AK or HI).

Designed by Hammond Hammond
Composition by Goodfellow and Egan Ltd, Cambridge
Printed and Bound by BPCC Hazell Books, Paulton and Aylesbury

10 9 8 7 6 5 4 3 2 1

This book is printed on acid-free paper.

First Published in Great Britain in 1991 by
Simon and Schuster Young Books

CONTENTS

INTRODUCTION

In the nineteenth century, the years between 1800 and 1900, people all over the world saw greater changes in their lives than anyone had ever seen before in history. These changes affected almost every part of life.

In 1800, the fastest way to travel was on horseback. By 1900, express trains ran between the major cities and the first cars could be seen on the roads. In 1800, sailors still relied on wind and wave power to cross the oceans. By 1900, the world's shipping was powered by steam. In 1800, most people worked in farming and lived in the countryside. By 1900, in Europe and North America, most worked and lived in towns and cities. In 1900, most people lived longer, healthier lives than their ancestors had done a century earlier. The way the world lived in 1800 had changed little for hundreds of years. Life in 1900 was much more like life today.

In Part One of this book you will read about how these changes began and how they affected the way people lived. You will see how one change, such as the invention of the steam engine, led to others, and how the chain of change went on and on, with one link in the chain leading to the next. You will notice something else, too. The chain of change began to draw countries together, so that what happened in one place could alter the lives of people on the other side of the world. For the first time, people began to realize something that they are still learning—that all human beings live on the same Earth and have to work out a way of sharing it.

In Part Two you will see how, as the nineteenth century went on, the world began to look more as it does today. The map of Europe became less dotted with tiny states as Germany and Italy became two nations. People in Europe and North America became more aware of the nations of the Far East and Africa. Many of the things that we take for granted today were invented, such as the electric light bulb, electric motors, the telephone and radio. But other, less welcome, changes were leading the world towards the wars of the twentieth century.

SWEDEN AND NORWAY

DENMARK

RUSSIA

UNITED KINGDOM

BERLIN

SAXONY

PARIS

FRANCE

AUSTRIAN EMPIRE

AUSTRIA

VIENNA

HUNGARY

PIEDMONT

OTTOMAN EMPIRE

PORTUGAL

SPAIN

KINGDOM OF SARDINIA

Europe in 1815

Prussian territories

Austrian Empire

Kingdom of Sardinia

PART ONE

The Old World

In 1792 the French had set out to conquer Europe. The wars that followed, known as the Napoleonic Wars, lasted more than 20 years and finally ended at the Battle of Waterloo in June 1815, when Austria, Britain, Prussia and Russia defeated the French. Afterwards, the European leaders held a long series of meetings in Vienna in Austria to work out a peace settlement. This series of meetings is known as the Congress of Vienna.

MAKING PEACE The Napoleonic Wars had been long and costly. The victors were determined that there would never be another war like them and they decided to divide Europe up so that no single country was strong enough to make war on the others as France had done. The Congress took no notice of what the people of Europe themselves wanted, which later led to trouble when the people of some of the smaller states fought for independence. But in one way the Congress was successful, for it was 100 years before another major war broke out in Europe.

RICH AND POOR The Congress of Vienna was a celebration as well as a conference. There were great banquets, balls and parties and the statesmen enjoyed themselves.

But life was not so good for the ordinary people of

Europe. Thousands of soldiers returning from the wars found it hard to get jobs. During the wars, many people had made their living by making or selling all kinds of war materials, from cannons to uniforms, and when peace came, they lost their jobs, too. Many other families had fled from their homes during the 20 years of battles and now had nowhere to live. In some countries, the war had ruined farmland and food was scarce.

THE THREAT OF REVOLUTION So behind the peace agreement and the celebrations there were many problems. Before the Napoleonic Wars, the French Revolution had toppled King Louis XVI (1774–1793), and other European rulers were terrified that there might be revolution in their own countries. The gap between rich and poor had been one of the causes of the French Revolution, and throughout Europe the gap was still there.

Yet, very gradually, another revolution had begun, although it was not the kind that rulers feared. This was the Industrial Revolution, which marked the change from farming to manufacturing as the main source of work and wealth. By 1900, the "old world" of Europe had become a group of industrial nations and industry had spread to the world's other continents.

Changes in Society
POVERTY AND PROTEST

Most wars cause more problems than they solve. The Napoleonic Wars between France and the rest of Europe were no different. When they were over, most of the people of Europe were living in misery.

War was not the only reason for their poverty. Another was that the number of people in Europe had almost doubled in the previous 100 years. People lived longer and had larger families. More children survived illness and grew up to become parents in their turn. This meant that more families were trying to make a living from the same amount of land.

RICH AND POOR Poor country families could not help noticing the difference between their lives and the lives of the landowners in their grand houses. Things were no better in the cities. Factory-owners and merchants lived in luxury while the people whose work made them wealthy had poor homes, poor pay and often not enough to eat. For many families there was no work at all and no money to live on. They had to go begging in the streets.

GOVERNMENTS How could things be changed? Ordinary people had no votes, so they could not bring about changes by voting for a different government. The French Revolution of 1789 was long over, but the ideas that had sparked it off lived on and spread. People wanted more say in how their countries were run. They wanted a share in the wealth of the rich. Countries that were part of foreign empires wanted their own rulers.

Areas of Revolution 1830–1848

- ● Centres of revolutionary activity 1830
- ● Centres of revolutionary activity 1840
- ▨ Areas of revolt 1830
- ▨ Areas of revolt 1848

In 1830 and 1848, the spirit of revolt spread from France through Europe. In 1848 it even reached the repressive regimes of Russia and the Ottoman Empire.

In Germany and Italy there was another problem. Each was made up of numbers of small states, some poor and some rich. Many Germans wanted *unification*—the joining of the German states into one Germany. Many Italians felt the same about Italy.

Some of the people of Austria wanted exactly the opposite. Austria was one country made up of many races with different languages and ways of life. Each of these groups wanted to govern themselves.

Napoleon, seen here at the head of his troops, had aimed to make the whole of Europe a French empire. When he was finally defeated, statesmen had to re-draw the map.

The Communist Manifesto

In 1848 two German writers published a book which was to change the way people thought about government. Karl Marx (1818–1883) and Frederick Engels (1820–1895) called their book *The Communist Manifesto*.

Marx and Engels believed that the time was coming when the people who did the work would rule. Statesmen and the rich owners of industries and land would be overthrown, and the workers would elect their own leaders. In 1848, it seemed for a while as if they might be right.

The Wars with France 1792–1815

1792 April: France declared war on Austria
1793 January: King Louis XVI executed. Britain and Spain unite war against France.
1799 Frightened by French successes in the war, Austria, Britain, Russia and Turkey joined forces. They were called the Allies
1802 Napoleon planned the invasion of Britain.
1805 The British navy defeated the French fleet at the Battle of Trafalgar, but the French army defeated the Austrians and Russians at Austerlitz
1812 Napoleon's army reached Moscow before being forced to retreat from Russia
1814 The Allies invaded France and forced Napoleon to abdicate as emperor
1815 Napoleon, imprisoned on the island of Elba, escaped and gathered a new army to fight the Allies. He was finally beaten at the Battle of Waterloo in June

REVOLUTION In 1830 and again in 1848, all these feelings boiled up into revolution in many parts of Europe. Monarchs and statesmen were frightened. They sent troops to attack the rioters and rebels, killing them or putting them in prison. The governments of other countries often helped these rulers, because they were afraid that if revolution succeeded in one country, it would spread to others.

The 1848 revolutions began in Paris when troops fired into a crowd of demonstrators. When news of this spread, there were riots in Austria, Italy and parts of Germany. In some places, revolution brought changes, but these made very little real difference to most people. The revolutionaries had no experience of power and started quarreling among themselves. Life continued as before, with the rich getting richer and the poor staying poor.

But ideas do not die. Writers and speakers went on saying that things must change and that all people, not just the rich, should decide how their country should be ruled. The struggle for *democracy*—votes for everyone and government by the people—had begun.

Peoples in the Austrian Empire 1848

The Austrian Empire, in 1848, brought together peoples who had no language, culture or religion in common. All sought their own nationhood.

German · Czech · Slovak · Italian · Hungarian · Slovenian · Russian · Croatian · Polish · Romanian

THE INDUSTRIAL REVOLUTION

Before the Industrial Revolution, most things were made using human energy. Cotton and woolen thread were spun on spinning wheels, which were turned by hand or foot. Thread was woven into cloth on *looms* operated in the same way. Blacksmiths used hammers to beat iron into tools. Wood was cut with handsaws.

The Industrial Revolution began gradually, late in the seventeenth century, when machines were invented to spin and weave cotton. At first these machines were driven by water power, but after about 1800 steam engines were used to make them work.

FACTORY LIFE By 1830 most cotton goods made in Britain were made in factories. Other countries followed Britain's lead and by 1850 Belgium, France, Germany, Italy and the United States of America were catching up. Meanwhile, many other industries—such as wool spinning and weaving, iron-making, brick-making, pottery and brewing—also began to start factory production using steam power.

Factory work meant a new kind of life for millions of people. Instead of working on their own or in small groups, they now worked alongside hundreds of other people. They could take a rest or a meal only when the factory owners said so. The working day was very long, sometimes 12 hours or more. Many factory workers were children, some as young as five or six years old. Four-year-olds were employed in some of Germany's linen mills.

There were two reasons for employing such young children. One was that they could be paid very low wages; the other was that they were small enough to crawl into machines that were still running. In the weaving industry, "piecing" was one of the jobs given to small children. When threads broke in the loom, the children had to climb in and join the threads together again. Every day they risked terrible injury or death.

Industry in Europe c1850

- ○ Coalfields
- ◇ Iron ore
- □ Textile industry

The Industrial Revolution began to develop in Britain and spread quite rapidly to the coal-mining areas of northwestern Europe over the next few years.

Left. Factory workers toiled in smoke, noise, grime and constant danger. This was the scene in a German iron foundry in 1875.

Above. Until 1842, young children were employed in British coal mines.

Left. The Davy lamp detected gas, but led to the sinking of deeper pits.

THE DEMAND FOR COAL Steam engines were fueled by coal. As the number of factories grew, so more coal was needed. Again, Britain led the development here and in 1830 it produced four-fifths of the world's coal. Much of it was sent to Europe to fuel the factories there. To find more coal, miners had to sink deeper and deeper pits. This was possible because steam engines could drive the lifts that carried the miners and the coal between the coal face and the surface. But in deep mines there was a greater danger of rockfalls, flooding or poisonous, explosive gas. During the nineteenth century, about 1,000 British miners were killed and over 150,000 seriously injured each year. In the early years of the Industrial Revolution, many of these were women and children.

MAKING WORK SAFER From about 1830, there were moves in some countries to make work in factories and mines safer. Working hours became shorter and there were laws to prevent young children being employed. But there were not enough inspectors to make sure that the law was being obeyed, and parents usually needed the wages that their children brought home.

Children at Work

Elizabeth Bentley started work in a cotton mill in 1815 when she was six years old. The work was dreadfully hard and the factory owners gave no thought to the safety of their employees or the conditions under which they worked. This is the story she told:

I worked from five or six in the morning till seven or nine at night. I had forty minutes for a meal at noon. At any other time, we had to eat or drink as we worked. If we got tired, the overlooker [man in charge] beat us with a strap. Sometimes we could not see each other for dust.

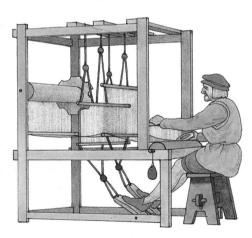

Above. Hand-loom weavers were thrown out of work by faster, cheaper factory weaving.

Below. The spinning wheel could not compete with the spinning machines in the factories.

THE COMING OF THE RAILWAYS

On 27 September 1825 there was great excitement in the towns of Stockton and Darlington in north east England. Everyone had the day off work and crowds gathered along the railway line that had been built between the two towns.

Soon, cheering could be heard along the line. Then a locomotive puffed into view, pulling more than 20 open wagons filled with passengers. They were the first passengers in the world to travel on a steam train.

THE RAILWAY AGE The Stockton to Darlington Railway was built mainly to carry coal from the mines at Darlington to the port at Stockton. But it showed that railways had a future for carrying passengers too. Soon, plans were made for more railways both in Britain and in other countries. America's first railway, the South Carolina Railroad, opened in 1830. The first French line was built in 1832 and Germany, Belgium, Russia and Italy followed. The Railway Age had begun. By the 1870s, all the main cities in Europe and in the eastern states of America were linked by rail.

The great advantage of rail transport was its speed. In the early nineteenth century, traveling by road, on horseback or in horse-drawn vehicles, was slow and uncomfortable. The fastest stagecoaches could only travel at 9.6 miles an hour and it took 18 hours to cover the 180 miles from London to Manchester.

The first train from Stockton to Darlington reached over 14.4 miles an hour and railway journeys at twice that speed were soon usual. In 1838 the

By 1875, railway travel for the rich had a touch of luxury. This Pullman car echoed the saloon of a Victorian country house with its plush furniture and decor. Servants were on call at the touch of a bell.

rail journey from London to Manchester took only 12 hours and within a few years it was even quicker.

RAILWAYS AND TRADE Railways made it possible for people to travel further to work, to visit friends and go on holiday. But it was the goods that were carried by trains that made most difference to people's lives. Carrying goods by rail was very much faster and cheaper than sending them by road or canal, so manufacturers built their factories near railway stations to take advantage of this. Towns near railways grew rapidly, for heavy goods such as bricks and coal could be carried there easily and cheaply. Milk, eggs and other fresh food could also be taken overnight from country towns to the cities.

There was another important result of railway-building. It used up huge amounts of iron and steel, and this led to the growth of the iron and steel industries in European countries and in the United States of America.

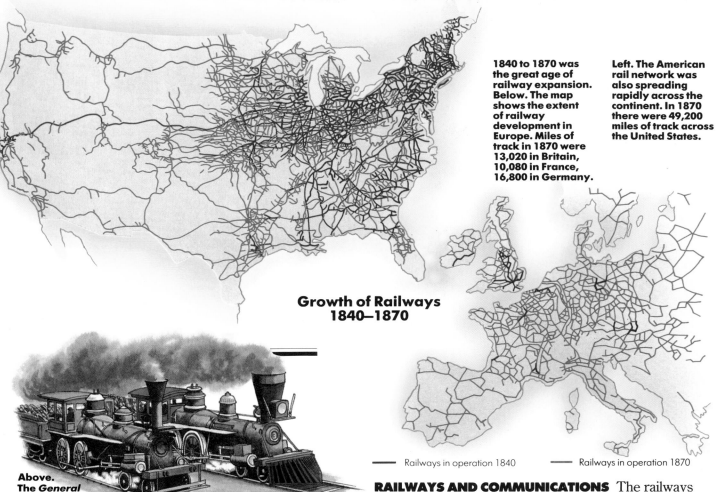

1840 to 1870 was the great age of railway expansion. Below. The map shows the extent of railway development in Europe. Miles of track in 1870 were 13,020 in Britain, 10,080 in France, 16,800 in Germany.

Left. The American rail network was also spreading rapidly across the continent. In 1870 there were 49,200 miles of track across the United States.

Growth of Railways 1840–1870

—— Railways in operation 1840   —— Railways in operation 1870

Above.
The *General* races against the *Texas*.

The General – Texas Chase

Railways were soon found useful for moving troops and equipment in wartime.

In the American Civil War of 1861–65 (see pages 36–37) there was a famous chase between two locomotives, the *General* and the *Texas*, driven by opposing sides. The plan was for the *General* to use explosives to blow up the line behind it, but the *Texas* kept so close that this was impossible. After a chase at a speed of 60 miles per hour, the *General* ran out of fuel and its crew was captured.

RAILWAYS AND COMMUNICATIONS The railways also brought a revolution in communications. As early as 1838, the governments of both Britain and the USA recognized railways as official carriers of the mail. Newspapers also began to be distributed by rail, which meant that copies could be carried overnight to places hundreds of miles from where they were printed.

The railways were also among the first users of telegraphy, which was invented in the 1840s (see page 68). In some countries, including Britain, the railway telegraph was used as a postal service to carry and deliver urgent messages in country areas.

The opening of the Stockton to Darlington Railway on 27 September 1825, the first railway in the world to carry passengers and goods. The train was headed by George Stephenson's *Locomotive Engine No 1*. The flag carried by the man in front bore the motto in Latin, "Through private danger to the public good." The violent jolting of the train may have made passengers reflect on these words! In 1829, Stephenson won the £500 prize in a competition to decide which locomotive would be used on the new Liverpool to Manchester line. His famous *Rocket* reached speeds of 33.6 miles per hour.

MANUFACTURERS AND MARKETS

Bales of raw cotton are loaded at Savannah, Georgia, for shipment to the mills of Europe.

and sailors to collect the raw cotton from abroad and then take the finished goods overseas again.

TRADE ACROSS THE WORLD

Countries depended more and more on one another for trade and a disturbance in one country could affect a trading partner thousands of miles away. For example, during the Napoleonic Wars of 1792 to 1815 (see page 9), the British and French navies interfered with each other's merchant ships, which affected world trade badly. The USA was one of the countries that suffered most and this led to war between the USA and Britain from 1812 to 1814.

The war was not a very serious conflict, but it put a stop to American overseas trade and led to high unemployment and many businesses going *bankrupt* in America. It also caused distress in the British cotton industry because the war interrupted supplies of raw American cotton.

After the Industrial Revolution began (see pages 12–13), factories made goods in larger numbers than ever before. This meant that they needed good supplies of *raw materials* such as cotton or iron to turn into manufactured products, and they also needed more customers to buy their products. Many raw materials came from abroad, and manufactured goods were sent abroad in exchange for them.

TRADING AROUND THE WORLD The Industrial Revolution brought a huge increase in trade between countries. We can see how this happened by taking just one industry as an example. British inventions had made the British cotton industry the world leader. Cotton cannot be grown in Britain, so British mills needed raw cotton from overseas to make into thread and then into cloth. Most of it came from America and India. Cotton cloth, and clothes made from it, were then sent abroad to be sold. So the cotton industry, as well as giving jobs to British factory workers, provided work for British ships

THE TRADING ROUNDABOUT Other industries grew as the cotton industry had, by importing raw materials from overseas and exporting goods manufactured from them. By 1850, half of the wool used in British mills came from Australia. Jute from India was turned into canvas goods. Iron and other metal ores all poured into Europe to be made into manufactured goods for export. European industrial machinery was used to produce even more raw materials in other countries, and so trade went on. Trade and industry were like the horses on a merry-go-round, speeding faster and faster.

When the trade merry-go-round was spinning fast, manufacturers made good profits and workers earned good pay. But sometimes the merry-go-round slowed down or stopped. If more goods were produced than could be sold, prices had to be cut, which in turn cut profits and pay. At other times, a poor harvest overseas could lead to a shortage of raw materials for the factories. For the first time in history, people's lives could be affected by something that happened on the other side of the world.

Business deals were made in "exchanges" which specialized in particular goods. This is the Corn Exchange in London. There, samples would be inspected and prices agreed.

1 The Industrial Revolution began in Britain but soon spread to France and Germany. At first, Britain tried to hold on to its lead by banning the export of machinery such as textile looms, but this was ended in 1843. Coal was the basic fuel for industry. World coal production increased by at least 60 percent every ten years between 1830 and 1880. Britain was the largest producer, turning out 86 million tons in 1860, compared with Germany's 21 and France's 10. Much of Britain's coal was exported to Europe.

Britain and France

In 1830, the world's two main trading nations were Britain and France. Britain's main imports — items brought in from abroad — were raw cotton, sugar, grains and tea. Its chief exports — those it sold overseas — were cotton and woolen thread and cloth, linen and cutlery.

France's principal imports were cotton, sugar, silk and animal skins.

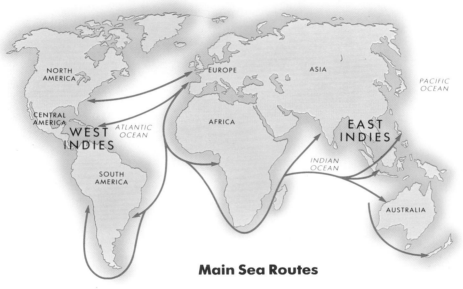

Main Sea Routes

2 The development of industry created a need for capital and a means of spreading the risk for investors. In Britain and France, and later in Germany, the principle of limited liability made investment less risky, and limited liability companies became the usual way of financing new enterprises.

Right. War broke out in 1812 between Britain and the USA over British attempts to prevent American ships trading in Europe. The battle of New Orleans was the last engagement of the war, which almost ruined the British cotton industry by cutting off supplies of raw materials.

Above. The world's main sea trading routes in the mid-nineteenth century, before the opening of the Suez Canal in 1869 which greatly shortened voyages between Europe and the East.

Coping with Change
LIFE IN THE CITIES

Typical housing in an industrial city. Each floor of these tenements would be occupied by a separate family. Their communal washhouses and lavatories were outside in the yard.

What was life like for factory workers in the growing industrial cities in Europe and North America?

HOUSING PROBLEMS Life was not very pleasant. The industrial cities grew very quickly. In 1851 the population of Bradford, the center of the British woolen industry, was four times what it had been in 1801. The American weaving city of Philadelphia, Pennsylvania, trebled its size during the same 50 years. Families who had come from the country to work in the factories were desperate for somewhere to live. A builder would buy a plot of land and try to cram as many homes as possible onto it, often building on damp, marshy land that was no use for anything else. Many houses were built "*back-to-back*" so that there was only one wall between two rows of houses.

Most homes were "two up, two down"—that is, there were two rooms (a kitchen and a living room) downstairs and two bedrooms upstairs. Families were large, often with ten or more children, so several children often had to share one bedroom and even one bed. Water came from a pump at the end of each row of houses. Several families shared a washhouse and lavatory. In some cities builders put up blocks of *tenements*, which were two-roomed apartments built several stories high.

The smell was terrible. There were no sewers to carry away dirty water and human waste, which simply drained away in the streets. There was no collection of trash, so this, too, was left to rot. Some families even kept their trash in their homes until they could stand the smell no longer! Rats, mice, flies, bugs and other vermin lived freely in the streets and houses.

DANGER AT WORK At work, there were other risks to health. Industries such as pottery, iron and brick-making produced *pollution* of all kinds. Smoke, dust and poisonous fumes belched out of factory chimneys. There was no control over the disposal of waste produced by

Above. Industrial cities grew so rapidly that many families had to crowd into single rooms with little furniture and no proper cooking or sanitary facilities. Left. New industrial housing was often built "back to back" to save space and materials. Shared lavatories for the whole terrace were built at the end of each row.

Above. How the rich lived. Increasingly, in the nineteenth century, the source of their wealth was industry. The hunger for coal and iron ore made fortunes for many landowners. Disraeli, the Prime Minister, commented that Britain had become two nations, rich and poor.

Many of Emile Zola's novels attacked the squalor of life in industrial France.

Charles Dickens began his working life in a factory and knew industry at first hand.

factories, so it often seeped into the ground and poisoned water supplies.

It is not surprising that when sickness broke out in the cities, it spread rapidly. Few factory workers could afford doctors, so they tried to cure their illnesses with cheap, useless medicines.

THE GREAT CHOLERA EPIDEMICS In the 1820s a dreadful disease spread throughout Asia and Europe from India. It was cholera. No-one knew how it spread, but by 1830 it had reached Russia and by 1831 had arrived in Germany, France and Britain. From Europe it traveled by ship to North America.

There was no cure. If you caught cholera, you would almost certainly die within a few days. In Russia in 1830, one in 20 people died of the disease, in Poland one in 30. In Belgium, the Netherlands and Britain, cholera killed about one person in every 130. In 1848 and 1854, the disease broke out again.

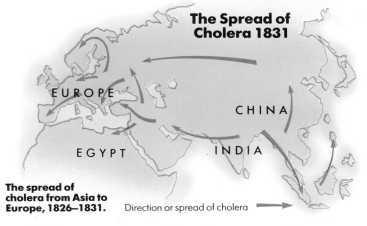

The Spread of Cholera 1831

The spread of cholera from Asia to Europe, 1826–1831.

Direction or spread of cholera ➝

Cholera was only one of the diseases spread by infected water, open drains and overcrowded homes. Other illnesses were caused by working conditions and pollution in the factories. People who lived in the industrial cities of the nineteenth century faced an unhealthy life and an early death.

THE PROTESTERS

A cartoon of the "Peterloo Massacre" in Manchester, Great Britain, in 1819. A peaceful protest was broken up by mounted troops and eleven protesters were killed.

The Industrial Revolution (see pages 12–13) changed the lives of millions of people, but for most of them change did not mean improvement. Although manufacturers, mine and shipowners, railway builders and merchants made fortunes, there were few rewards for the people who worked for them. Their work had created a new kind of society, but they had no say in how it was to be run. In most countries, government was in the hands of small groups of powerful people. An exception was the United States of America, which had a form of democracy (for white men only) from 1801. In some countries such as Russia, the ruler had absolute power and no-one could question what he or she did.

STUDENTS AND CRAFTSPEOPLE In every country there were people who were determined that something must be done to improve life for the workers. Their aim was democracy—government by the people. In Germany, France and Italy, students held meetings and produced newspapers demanding democracy. Students were among the leaders of the revolutions of 1830 and 1848 (see page 11). Marx and Engels (see page 25) worked out their first political ideas at university.

In Britain, students had to be more careful in what

they said or wrote because if they upset the universities, they would be told to leave. This meant that in Britain the protesters tended to be craftspeople like weavers and printers. Some formed a society called the Chartists, which wanted all adult men to have the vote so that ordinary people would be represented in *Parliament*. But they never gained enough supporters to bring about any change.

CONTROLLING IDEAS
Governments and their armies were too strong for the revolutionaries, as the events of 1830 and 1848 showed. Governments also did all they could to stop the spread of new ideas. In 1819 the German states agreed to *censor* magazines and newspapers, ban political meetings and keep a check on anyone with "dangerous" opinions. In Italy, the leaders of protest movements were forced to go abroad to escape punishment, and until 1847 newspapers were censored.

In Britain, *trade unions*—groups of workers joining together to demand better pay or working conditions—were banned until 1824. Even ten years later, six British farm workers were sent to a prison camp in Australia because they tried to form a union. Another way of controlling ideas in Britain was the heavy tax on newspapers that was the law till 1855. This meant that only the rich could afford them, so newspapers only printed news that the rich wanted to read.

THE UNDERGROUND PRESS These restrictions held back the movement for reform, but they did not completely stop it. In most European countries there were presses operating "underground," meaning that they secretly printed illegal newspapers, pamphlets and books despite the risk of police raids and imprisonment.

Slowly, governments came to see that it was better to accept some reforms than to risk revolution and bloodshed. All Frenchmen were given the vote in 1851 and Britain gave votes to an increasing number of men as time went on.

Voices of Protest

Giuseppe Mazzini (1805–1872) planned to make his career in law, but after leaving Genoa University he founded an organization called Young Italy whose aim was to unite all the Italian states under a *republican* government. Young Italy was involved in the revolutions of 1830 and 1848, but Mazzini himself spent much of his life in *exile*. He lived to see Italy unified — but under a king and not as a republic.

Louis Kossuth (1802–1894) was a journalist who led a movement in Hungary that wanted democratic reform and freedom from Austrian control. He was imprisoned for what he wrote, but after he was released he continued to write pamphlets, which were either illegally printed or copied out by hand. In 1847 Kossuth was elected to the Hungarian parliament and he became a leader of the 1848 Hungarian revolt. This failed, and he spent the rest of his long life in exile.

**Above. German cavalry ride against protesters.
Right. Italian patriot Giuseppe Mazzini.
Far right. British Chartist leader Feargus O'Connor.**

Feargus O'Connor (1794–1855) became leader of the Chartist movement in Britain. The Chartists wanted all men to be able to vote in a *secret ballot* at annual elections to Parliament. They organized three *petitions*, in 1839, 1842 and 1848, which contained these and other demands. O'Connor was a brilliant speaker and ran a Chartist newspaper called *The Northern Star*. But when he died the Chartist movement died with him.

Left. Producing an underground newspaper in a German cellar. Police raids meant that many such papers were short-lived, but they would often be started up again in new hiding places.

Literature of Dissent

1791 Tom Paine's *The Rights of Man*

1840 Giuseppe Mazzini's *The Duties of Man*
1848 *The Communist Manifesto*
1859 John Stuart Mill's *On Liberty*
1867 Karl Marx's *Capital*

CRISIS IN THE COUNTRYSIDE

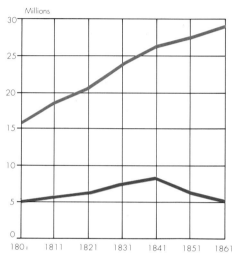

British and Irish Populations 1801–1861

Millions

Left. Starving families seek food and shelter at an Irish workhouse in 1846. So many people needed help that the workhouses could not cope with the demand and people were turned away to die in the streets.

Above. This graph of the population of the British Isles from 1801 to 1861 shows how the Great Famine hit Ireland. Even today, the Irish population has not returned to its 1861 level.

Until about 1830, the main industry in Europe and North America, and in the rest of the world, was farming. Most people lived and worked in small farming communities. Their work was hard and their pay was poor, they ate simple food and lived in cramped, often damp houses. Life was not easy for farm workers, but they were able to survive. The most prosperous farm workers in Europe were the French. Many had their own small plots of land for crops and could keep animals on pasture that was shared with others.

MOVING TO THE CITIES At the time of the Industrial Revolution (see pages 12–13), all this began to change. Farm machinery was too expensive for small farm owners in France to buy. In other countries, the use of farm machinery meant that fewer farm workers were needed. If farm workers lost their jobs, they also lost their houses, which were owned by the farmers. There was no pay for people who were out of work. All they

could do was to move somewhere else to look for work.

Throughout the nineteenth century there was a great movement of people from the country to the towns, where the new factories could provide jobs and homes were available nearby. It was usually the younger and fitter families who moved. Old people, the sick, the disabled and the very poor who could not afford to move were left behind in the countryside. For them, life became even harder. They had to take any work they could find, for any wage the farmers would pay. Farmers often gave work to women and children, who were paid less than men.

THE GREAT FAMINE Then, in 1845, there was another blow. The main food of country people in many parts of Europe was potatoes. In 1845, a disease called blight attacked the potato crop, turning the potatoes black and rotten. Food became desperately short. The famine was worst in Ireland, where almost one million Irish people

Above. This idealized view of an Irish croft may have been true to life before 1845. Things changed after the famine, however, and many families starved to death.

Right. Before the invention of the threshing machine, threshing corn with a flail provided work for farm laborers through the winter.
Left. The threshing machines robbed the men of weeks of work because they could do the job more quickly and with fewer workers.

1 Population figures for Europe's major cities show how they were a magnet for people from the countryside. Between 1801 and 1851 the populations of Berlin and St. Petersburg increased by over 140 percent, London by 127 percent, and Paris and Vienna by over 80 percent.

2 Europe was not the only part of the world with a rapidly increasing population. There are no fully reliable world population figures for the nineteenth century, but it has been estimated that between 1845 and 1914 the number increased from 1 billion to 1.9 billion. This huge increase brought problems to many societies. In Africa, for example, tribes were forced to find — or fight for — new land to feed their growing numbers as their own land became degraded by overcultivation.

The Threshing Machine

The increasing use of machinery in farming meant less work for families who stayed in the countryside. The first important development was the threshing machine, which separated grain from the straw. This was invented by a Scotsman called Andrew Meikle in 1786 and by the early nineteenth century it was widely used.

Previously, threshing had been done by hand, using *flails* to beat the corn on the threshing floor of the barn, and farm workers had relied on this work in the winter to provide them with jobs when other work was scarce. Now the threshing machine, which was driven by horses or water at first and later by steam, did in a few days the work that used to occupy many workers for months. The result was that there was very little work available after the harvest, and in those days the rule was: "No work, no pay."

starved to death over the next two years. But the picture was similar all over Europe, especially in Germany. Despite the numbers who had moved to the towns, there were still too many people trying to make a living from the land.

FEEDING EUROPE The Great Famine of the 1840s was really part of a much wider problem. Since the eighteenth century, the population of Europe had been growing. In 1830 it was about 230 million, almost twice what it had been 100 years earlier. Farm machinery had increased the production of food, but not enough to feed the extra numbers of people. In the early part of the nineteenth century, many people feared that Europe would face starvation in a few years' time.

There were two possible answers to the problem. One was for some of the people in Europe to move to other parts of the world. The other was for Europe to find new sources of food. Both of these things happened.

RUSSIA: THE SLEEPING GIANT

In 1800, the world was changing fast. War was altering the boundaries of European countries. The United States of America, which had only just been founded, was growing in power and wealth. Australia and New Zealand were about to be developed by settlers from Europe. But between Europe and Asia lay a sleeping giant that was still part of the old world of the *Middle Ages*. This was Russia.

AN UNCHANGING SOCIETY Russia did not have an elected government. It was ruled by an emperor called the tsar, with an army of officials to carry out his orders.

The agricultural and industrial revolutions in western Europe had passed Russia by. About half of its population were still *serfs*. They were the property of the person who owned the land on which they lived and worked.

Russia had expanded its control to the east as far as the Pacific Ocean, but there were not enough people to settle in this huge area and the Russians knew nothing of the technology needed to develop it. So the occupation of central Asia required a large army to fight constant battles against the tribes of the region.

Russia's problems were made worse by the cruelty, violence and even madness of the tsars. Tsar Paul I (1796–1801) refused to take advice from his officials and combined cruelty at home with disastrous policies abroad. He was finally murdered and his son Alexander (1801–1825), who had taken part in the murder plot, took over.

In 1812 the French army invaded Russia and reached as far as Moscow before being defeated. After the final defeat of France in 1815 (see page 11), Tsar Alexander

Russian Empire in Asia to 1900

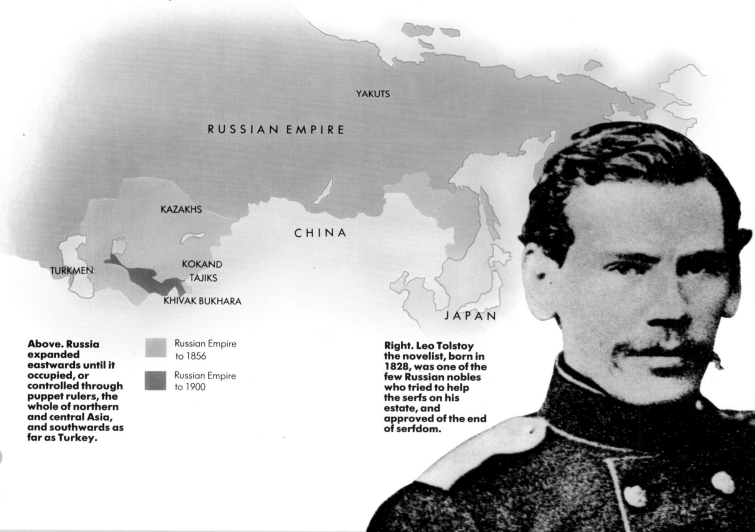

YAKUTS

RUSSIAN EMPIRE

KAZAKHS

CHINA

TURKMEN

KOKAND
TAJIKS

KHIVAK BUKHARA

JAPAN

Above. Russia expanded eastwards until it occupied, or controlled through puppet rulers, the whole of northern and central Asia, and southwards as far as Turkey.

Russian Empire to 1856

Russian Empire to 1900

Right. Leo Tolstoy the novelist, born in 1828, was one of the few Russian nobles who tried to help the serfs on his estate, and approved of the end of serfdom.

lived in fear of revolution and any talk of reform was forbidden. He set up a network of spies and secret police to report on any threat to his rule.

Alexander was succeeded by his brother Nicholas I (1825–1855), who trusted no-one. It was said that he made himself do with as little sleep as possible so that he would not be murdered in his bed. He had been trained as a soldier and believed in strict military discipline for everyone, soldiers and civilians.

THE CRIMEAN WAR One of Russia's problems was that it had very limited access to the sea, which prevented it from playing a full part in world trade. The ports on its northern coast froze up in winter and could not be used. Russians had always wanted to be able to reach the Mediterranean, but Turkey was in the way.

Tsar Nicholas's plan to take over Turkey led to the Crimean War in 1854, in which Britain and France joined to defend Turkey. The war ended in 1856 with Russia defeated, but by that time Nicholas I had died.

NEW REFORMS The next tsar, Alexander II (1855–1881), saw that reform was needed if Russia was to catch up with the rest of the world. He began by freeing the

Ill-fed, ill-housed and treated like beasts of burden, Russian serfs lived lives of unremitting hard work and misery.

serfs, who were then able to move from the land to the cities. This in turn made it possible for Russian industry to develop and forced farmers to adopt more modern methods of agriculture, using machinery. The sleeping giant began to awaken.

Left. Tsar Alexander II reads his proclamation abolishing serfdom in 1861. This was one of his many reforms that brought Russia closer to the modern world. He also improved education, administration and military organization. People resented his autocratic rule, however, and he was eventually assassinated.

The Trans-Siberian Railway 1890

RUSSIAN EMPIRE

LAKE BAIKAL

• CHITA

VLADIVOSTOK

CHINA

KOREA

— Route of railway

The Exploration of Siberia

Russia had no need to go overseas to find an empire. To the east lay the huge undeveloped land of Siberia, which was rich in resources such as timber, furs and minerals. Explorers from Russia had traveled in Siberia since the seventeenth century, and more recently a chain of forts had been set up to police the area. But there were too few people in Siberia to develop its resources and because most of its rivers ran north to the frozen Arctic they could only be used to transport timber and minerals for a few summer months. Until the building of the Trans-Siberian Railway at the end of the nineteenth century, Siberia's resources were hardly touched. hardly touched.

Right. British forces fighting in the Crimea went through terrible suffering from injury and disease. Their plight inspired Florence Nightingale (in the center) to take a team of volunteer nurses to set up proper hospitals in Turkey and to devote the rest of her life to nursing.

The Wider World
BUILDING EMPIRES

Hudson Bay, in northern Canada, in the early nineteenth century. The Hudson's Bay Company controlled all trade in fur from the Atlantic to the Pacific.

Soon after Europeans had made their voyages of discovery to distant parts of the world in the fifteenth and sixteenth centuries, they began to take over these lands for themselves. By 1800 the British, French, Spanish, Portuguese and Dutch all had empires overseas.

THE BRITISH EMPIRE By the 1820s Britain had by far the largest empire, with the strongest navy in the world to protect trade and travelers going to and from its colonies. In 1783, Britain had lost its American colonies in the American War of Independence, but it still had Canada. In 1788 the British also claimed Australia as their territory.

After the defeat of France in 1815 (see page 11), Britain took over Cape Colony in South Africa from the Dutch, and French islands in the Caribbean. India was ruled by the British, too, and there was also a scattering of small British islands across the South Atlantic and the Indian oceans. In 1840 New Zealand was added to the British Empire.

But although this empire looked huge on a map of the world, most of the countries it included had small populations and much of the land had not been explored by Europeans. It was not until the middle of the nineteenth century that the vast territories of Canada and Australia began to be settled and developed by large numbers of Europeans.

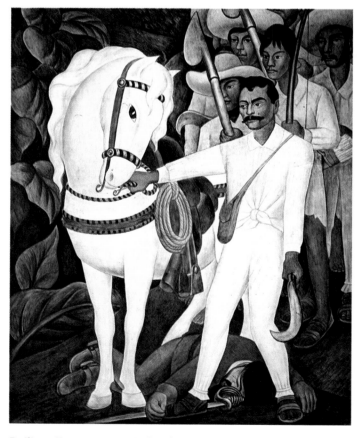

Emiliano Zapata was an Indian farmer who led an Indian struggle to recover their land in Mexico.

European Empires in 1870

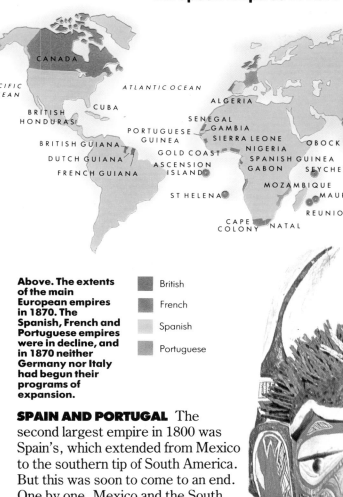

Above. The extents of the main European empires in 1870. The Spanish, French and Portuguese empires were in decline, and in 1870 neither Germany nor Italy had begun their programs of expansion.

- British
- French
- Spanish
- Portuguese

Growth of the British Empire 1760–1860

1763 Britain took Canada away from French control.
1767 British troops defeated the French in India and gradually expanded the area controlled by Britain
1788 The first British convict settlement was set up in Australia, soon followed by settlers who were not convicts
1795 British troops occupied the Cape of Good Hope at the southern tip of Africa
1808 Sierra Leone, in West Africa, became a British colony
1815 By the Treaty of Vienna, Britain gained the Cape (South Africa), Ceylon (Sri Lanka), Mauritius, Malta and French possessions in the Caribbean
1829 Britain claimed the whole of Australia as part of the Empire
1830 The Gold Coast (Ghana) came under British "protection"
1840 New Zealand became part of the British Empire
1842 Britain occupied Hong Kong
1843 The Gambia, in West Africa, became a British colony
1860 Lagos (Nigeria) became part of the Empire

Empire travel made Europe aware of other cultures. Left. A decorated figure from Papua New Guinea. Above. An African stool carved from solid wood.

SPAIN AND PORTUGAL

The second largest empire in 1800 was Spain's, which extended from Mexico to the southern tip of South America. But this was soon to come to an end. One by one, Mexico and the South American states fought for their independence. By 1824 the once-powerful Spanish Empire only contained the islands of Cuba and Puerto Rico in the Caribbean.

Brazil had never been part of the Spanish Empire, but belonged to Portugal. It became independent in 1820, leaving Portugal with only a few scattered colonies such as Goa in India.

CHANGING ATTITUDES TO EMPIRES

There are two ways of building an empire. One is to take over and rule a country that already has a large population and a settled government. This is what had happened in India. The other is to lay claim to a land where few people live, say that the country is "empty" and send settlers to live there.

In 1815, Britain had no intention of expanding its empire. Many Britons thought that overseas colonies were a nuisance. The American War of Independence had been a costly blow, while holding on to India involved keeping a large and expensive army there, as well as naval forces to protect the trading routes. It was hard to see how an empire could help Britain's wealth.

This attitude changed as the Industrial Revolution got under way (see pages 12–13). Colonies could provide cheap raw materials for British factories and, once settlers had arrived in those colonies, new markets for manufactured goods as well. At the same time, the empire offered homes and work for Britain's increasing population. So, from about 1840 onwards, the British began to take an interest in expanding their empire. This was to lead them into conflict later in the century with other European countries that had the same idea.

THE BRITISH IN INDIA

Above. Reinforcements arrive to relieve Lucknow, where the British had been surrounded by 60,000 Indians. This marked the end of the 1857 Indian Mutiny.

Above right. A cartoonist comments on British attitudes, represented by Queen Victoria, to India.

Right. Life for British families living in India was one of luxury. Here, boar hunters take a break for lunch.

"NEW CROWNS FOR OLD ONES!"

The first European traders to reach India were the Portuguese in 1498. They were followed by Dutch, French and British expeditions. The Portuguese and Dutch were interested in India only as a trading post, but the French and British had grander ideas. By 1767 the British had defeated the French and had begun to take over all of India. British India included the areas which are now the separate countries of Pakistan and Bangladesh.

THE EAST INDIA COMPANY British control of India was in the hands of the East India Company, which had been set up in 1600. The company had its own army, with British officers and mostly Indian troops. By the end of the eighteenth century the company had become so powerful that the British government became alarmed and sent several regiments of the regular British army to India to share the company's power.

India was a long way away from Britain and communications were slow. The commanders of the company and British armies could do more or less as they liked, setting themselves up as rulers of large areas. They interfered with the *Hindu* and *Muslim* religions of

India and tried to make the local people follow European ways and ideas. They spent money on roads, ports and industry—but this was for the benefit of trade, not to help the Indian people. The British officers lived well and enjoyed hunting large animals and other sports. They treated India as if it was a vast estate providing them with wealth and an unlimited supply of servants.

MUTINY OR REBELLION? Indian resentment of the British grew until it exploded into violence in 1857. This began in the army, when Indian troops in Bengal in northern India refused to obey the orders of their British officers. British historians still call this the period of the Indian *Mutiny*, but to Indian historians it was the "Great Rebellion" or "The Great War of Independence." For the next year there were outbreaks of violence all over northern India. British soldiers and their families were

British India 1805

Right. British possessions in India in 1805. The East India Company had gradually extended its power by making deals with local princes in areas where it was profitable to trade.

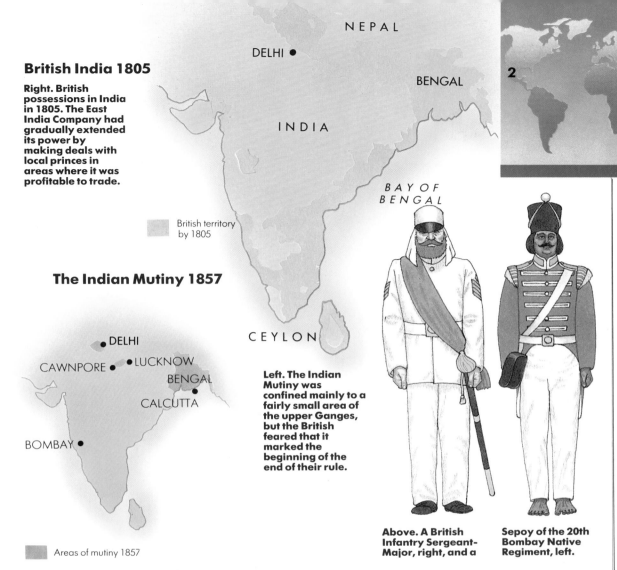

NEPAL

DELHI •

BENGAL

INDIA

BAY OF BENGAL

CEYLON

British territory by 1805

The Indian Mutiny 1857

• DELHI

CAWNPORE • • LUCKNOW

BENGAL

CALCUTTA •

BOMBAY •

Areas of mutiny 1857

Left. The Indian Mutiny was confined mainly to a fairly small area of the upper Ganges, but the British feared that it marked the beginning of the end of their rule.

Above. A British Infantry Sergeant-Major, right, and a

Sepoy of the 20th Bombay Native Regiment, left.

1 Apart from its importance as a source of raw materials and a market for finished goods, India was important to the shipping trade. Its importance increased after the introduction of steamships in the mid-19th century. Steamships traveling to the Far East and Australasia needed bunkering stations, where they took on supplies of coal, and Bombay was well-placed for this. After the opening of the Suez Canal in 1869 ships heading east found India even more convenient for bunkering.

2 Mexico is the largest of the Central American countries. In 1821 it became independent of Spain, which had colonized Mexico for 300 years, but there was an attempted Spanish invasion eight years later. From 1846—48 Mexico was at war with the United States. Defeat was followed by the loss of more than half Mexico's territory to the United States. In 1863 the French invaded and there was a war which lasted four years.

The Indian Mutiny 1857–1858

10 May 1857 At Meerut, 85 sepoys imprisoned. Others mutiny and march to Delhi

11 May 1857 Sepoys capture Delhi

4 June 1857 Sepoys at Cawnpore mutiny

24 June 1857 British at Cawnpore surrender. Rebels kill the troops and take the women and children prisoner

30 June 1857 British besieged at Lucknow

16 July 1857 British retake Cawnpore, find that all women and children have been murdered

14 Sept. 1857 British recapture Delhi

16 March 1858 Rebels at Lucknow defeated

19 June 1858 Rebel army defeated at Gwalior

attacked and murdered by the rebels. The worst violence was at Cawnpore, where over 600 British troops were murdered after they had surrendered, and the rebels then turned on their wives and children.

The British, afraid that they might lose control of India altogether, behaved just as violently in return. The rebels were ruthlessly hunted down, and by July 1858 the Mutiny had been quelled. India would have to wait for another 90 years before it gained its independence from Britain.

AFTER THE MUTINY The Mutiny had shaken the British, who now decided that the government would rule India directly, instead of through the East India Company. The army was strengthened and a new Indian Civil Service, with British staff, was set up to run the country. The system set up after 1858 lasted until India became independent in 1947.

Under direct British rule, India became the "jewel in the crown" of the British Empire, with good transport and successful industries. But almost all the benefits went to Britain, and the Indians became more and more resentful of the occupation of their country by a foreign army.

THE GREAT MIGRATIONS

In 1850, Britain controlled large areas of the world where the population was small compared to the size of the land. These areas included Canada, the whole of Australia away from the coast, and New Zealand.

The countries of the British Empire were not the only ones which seemed to offer opportunities to European settlers hungry for land to farm. There were vast areas of the United States of America that seemed almost unoccupied compared to overcrowded Europe. In South America, the countries that had won their independence from Spain also welcomed newcomers from Europe.

Above. A familiar dockside scene in nineteenth-century Britain, as relatives say goodbye to their emigrating loved ones. Many families decided to go to America to find work.

Left. Conditions on the emigrant ships were far from comfortable.

A FLOOD OF EMIGRANTS A steady trickle of *emigrants* leaving Europe for North and South America, Australia and New Zealand began before 1846, but after that the trickle quickly grew into a flood. The emigrants included many thousands of Irish and German families who had escaped the Great Famine (see pages 22–23) and were hoping to start a new life in the USA.

In North America, many of these people found work and homes in the growing industrial cities of the east. Others took the trail westwards to begin farming there. Like the emigrants to Australia and New Zealand, they sent home news of cheap—sometimes free—land, good crops and healthy living.

Many organizations offered to lend emigrants the fare for the journey, which they could pay back from their first earnings in their new country. Even so, it was a big decision to make. The fare from Britain to New Zealand, for example, was £18 for an adult, which was almost a year's wages for a farm worker. The fare for a child was £10, so two adults and three children (a small family in those days) needed more than £50 to get there.

Emigrants from Britain

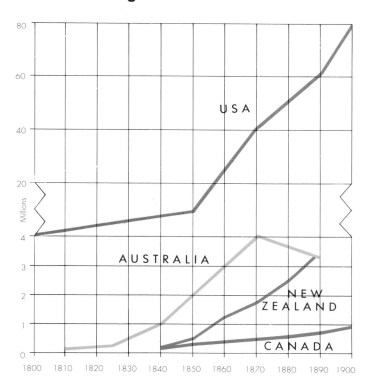

USA

AUSTRALIA

NEW ZEALAND

CANADA

HERE   AND   THERE;
OR, EMIGRATION A REMEDY.

Above. Emigration was put forward as a cure for poverty — but the really poor had no money for the fare.

Left. A view of Vancouver Harbor in 1876, just before it began to develop.

Above. This graph showing the destinations of emigrants from Britain between 1853 and 1912 reveals a changing pattern, with Canada gaining in popularity after 1903. This followed the completion of the Canadian Pacific Railway in 1885 which opened up the interior.

DANGEROUS VOYAGES Some of the ships used for emigrants had previously been used as slave ships, and conditions were almost as cramped as they had been for slaves. The voyage from Britain to New Zealand took 80 days. In the year 1847 alone, 17,000 emigrants to Canada died of "ship's fever" (typhus) either during or after the journey.

Once they had arrived in their new country, the farming emigrants had to "break in" the land, using only hand tools to make farmland out of scrub or bush. Many gave up the idea of having their own farms and went to work for the larger farmers instead. But others succeeded and became large farmers themselves.

An advertisement inviting immigrants to settle in California.

THE DESERTED VILLAGE The people of Bodney in Norfolk in eastern England were part of this great adventure. In 1855 the Oakley family, including five children, set out for Tasmania. Two years later the minister of the village's Methodist chapel organized a group of about 50 people— almost the whole village—to follow them. Most of the adults who went were young people in their 20s and 30s. Only the old and the sick were left behind.

When they arrived in Tasmania, they settled in an area which became known as "Norfolk Creek." Some families built up large farms. Others gave up farming and went off in search of gold, which had just been found in Tasmania. Their home village of Bodney gradually became deserted and almost disappeared, but for the people who got away there was new life and new hope.

THE AMERICAN WEST

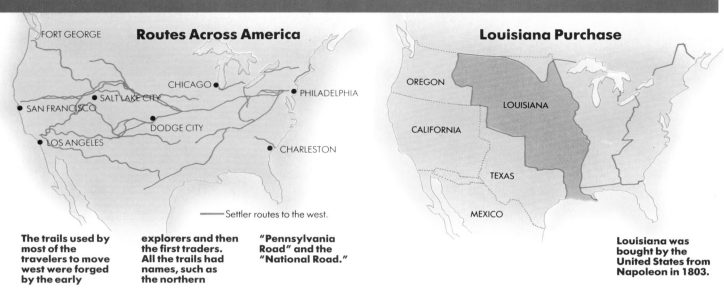

Routes Across America

FORT GEORGE
CHICAGO
SALT LAKE CITY
PHILADELPHIA
SAN FRANCISCO
DODGE CITY
LOS ANGELES
CHARLESTON

—— Settler routes to the west.

The trails used by most of the travelers to move west were forged by the early explorers and then the first traders. All the trails had names, such as the northern "Pennsylvania Road" and the "National Road."

Louisiana Purchase

OREGON
LOUISIANA
CALIFORNIA
TEXAS
MEXICO

Louisiana was bought by the United States from Napoleon in 1803.

The first Europeans to settle in North America made their new homes in the eastern states. Few people traveled west of the Mississippi River or the Great Lakes. But as more travelers ventured westwards, they brought back news of good farming country. From about 1820 onwards, thousands of families decided to go west to seek their fortunes. They settled in the western states of the United States and Canada.

WAGON TRAINS For safety, families traveled together in wagon trains. There were dozens of ox-drawn covered wagons in each train, led by a captain who had made the journey before. The *pioneers* had to take everything with them—food, clothes, bedding, tools, even furniture. There were no shops where they were going.

The journey west took several months, for wagon trains traveled slowly. They kept to fixed trails, but there were no roads or even tracks. It could take a day to travel 9 miles or cross a river. If a wheel broke, the whole train had to stop until it was mended. At night, the captain chose a place to camp and the men moved the wagons into a circle while the women cooked a meal over camp fires. Then the men took turns to watch for wild animals or attacking Indians while the others slept.

PIONEER LIFE Once the settlers had found a place to farm, life was no easier. First they had to make a clearing in the forest and build their homes out of the timber from the trees they had cut. They they had to dig up the tree

The California Gold Rush

News of the discovery of gold brought over 80,000 people to California in 1849 alone. They came over land along the pioneer trail or by sea round Cape Horn. At one time, there were 500 ships in San Francisco Bay whose crews had deserted to go and search for gold.

Most of the miners had come to California without their families. There was nothing to do except work and drink. The result was that California became the most lawless of the American states for many years.

Left. The movement of settlers to the American West was not good news for the indigenous Amerindian population, whose land was simply taken from them. They were treated as having no rights whatsoever and when they protested, they were mercilessly hunted down.

Right. The bison, too, was a victim of the pioneers. While the Indians had only hunted it to provide for their immediate needs, the new settlers hunted it almost to extinction.

roots to clear the land before they could plough it. There was no time or energy to do anything but work, except when winter snow drove the families indoors. In the early days there were no towns and there were few chances for people to get together. There were no doctors or hospitals, no teachers or schools. The pioneers' lives centered around their own families and they rarely saw anyone else.

The pioneers thought that the land was theirs to take—but it was not. The native Americans, or Amerindians were there already. At first, the local people were willing to share with the settlers, but many of the pioneers treated the Amerindians like animals and hunted them down, so the local people fought back. Sometimes they attacked the wagon trains. Sometimes

they waited until the pioneers were settled in their lonely farms and then they attacked. In the end the pioneers won, but the story of the destruction of the Amerindian nation is one of the most terrible in American history.

GOLD FEVER In 1848 came exciting news from California, in the west. Gold had been discovered. The next year, thousands of families set out on the California trail. Most prospectors searching for gold were unlucky, although the "Gold Rush" of 1849 brought fortunes to a few people. But the "Forty-niners," as they were called, had opened up the trail to California and thousands more families followed them to settle on the Pacific coast.

The pioneers depended entirely on themselves and their families for food and shelter. As soon as their grueling journey was over, they had to set about building a home and clearing the land. They had to bring all their equipment (right) with them. This included cooking utensils, furniture and farming implements as well as the few clothes and household items they possessed.

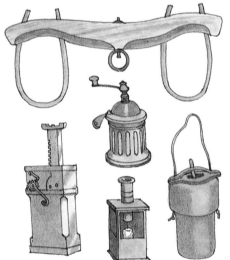

ENDING THE SLAVE TRADE

In 1800, millions of people in North and South America and the West Indies were slaves. They or their parents or grandparents had been hunted and captured in West Africa, packed into ships like cattle and then brought to be sold in the markets of the *New World*. From there, they were taken to work in places such as the tobacco, rice, sugar or cotton *plantations* in the southern states of the United States of America. In South America, slaves were put to work in the gold and silver mines. Slaves were also kept by the Dutch in South Africa and the Dutch East Indies, as well as by other countries.

Anti-slave trade engraving from 1890

NOTHING OF THEIR OWN French, British and Spanish settlers in the American continents had introduced slavery there early in the seventeenth century. By 1850 there were about four million slaves in the southern USA alone. There were a few kindly slave owners, but most worked their slaves hard, driving them on with whips and punishing them cruelly for minor offences.

Slaves and their families belonged to their owners. So did a slave's home and all their possessions. Owners encouraged the women to have children to increase the number of slaves they owned. They hunted down and tortured any slaves who escaped.

THE MIDDLE PASSAGE Slavery made the fortunes of many European ship-owners. They sailed to Africa with cargoes of goods to exchange with tribal chiefs in return for slaves. The second part of the voyage was called the Middle Passage and it took the slaves across the Atlantic Ocean to the Americas. On the return journey the ships would carry cotton or tobacco from America to Europe. Many European ports, including Liverpool and Bristol in Britain and Nantes in France, owed their wealth to this three-way trade.

Conditions on the slave ships were terrible. Slaves were packed tightly together, fastened in their places with iron chains. Many died on the voyage. Sometimes the sick were thrown overboard when they were still alive to prevent the spread of disease.

BANNING SLAVERY During the eighteenth century, protests had begun in Europe against this trade in human beings. One by one, European countries with overseas *colonies* banned the trade. Denmark was first, in 1802. The French, Dutch, Portuguese, Swedes and British followed, but slaves who were already in the colonies were not set free until later. It was 1838 before the British Empire freed all its slaves. This left just one major nation with large numbers of slaves—the USA. There, the cotton farmers of

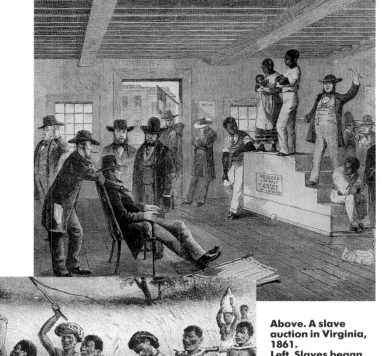

Above. A slave auction in Virginia, 1861.
Left. Slaves began their journey to America in Africa, where they were sold to European traders by tribal chiefs. The traders treated the Africans as a commodity, not as fellow human beings.

The Abolitionists

William **Wilberforce** (1759–1833) was the leader of the movement to abolish slavery in the British Empire. He was elected to Parliament in 1780 and began his campaign soon after that. Britain was involved in slavery in two ways. Not only did slaves do most of the work in the British colonies, but British ships and crews also played a leading part in the slave trade with other countries, especially the USA.

Wilberforce devoted much of his life to fighting slavery, but progress was slow. In 1807 a law was passed banning the slave trade in the British Empire, but there were 750,000 slaves already living there who were not freed. Finally in 1833, the year of Wilberforce's death, all the slaves in Britain were set free and five years later the slaves in British colonies were freed too.

Harriet Beecher Stowe (1811–1896) was brought up in Cincinatti, Ohio in the USA. There was no slavery in Ohio, but slaves from the neighboring state of Kentucky often escaped across the Ohio River. In 1852, Beecher Stowe published *Uncle Tom's Cabin*, a story

Right, Harriet Beecher Stowe. Below, William Wilberforce.

that told of the terrible conditions under which slaves lived and worked. Her book persuaded thousands of Americans that slavery should be abolished and when it was published in Europe it encouraged European opposition to American slavery.

the southern states depended on slave labor to plant, pick and harvest the crop.

As long as there was a demand for slaves in North America, some shipowners were willing to risk supplying that demand. A "pirate" slave trade continued, despite anti-slavery patrols by the ships of European navies.

Treatment of the slaves was worse than ever. At least two slave captains threw hundreds of slaves overboard when they sighted patrol boats. The only way of ending the Atlantic slave trade forever was to abolish slavery in the United States. This did not happen until 1865.

Slaves picking cotton in the southern US. Planters lived in grand style, for which slaves were essential. Some owners were very cruel, others treated their slaves kindly.

THE UNITED STATES DIVIDED

The North-South Divide

WASHINGTON TERRITORY

OREGON

NEVADA

NEBRASKA TERRITORY

UTAH TERRITORY

NEW MEXICO TERRITORY

MINNESOTA

WISCONSIN

MICHIGAN

IOWA

KANSAS

MISSOURI

INDIAN TERRITORY

ARKANSAS

TEXAS

LOUISIANA

ILLINOIS

INDIANA

OHIO

KENTUCKY

TENNESSEE

MISSISSIPPI

ALABAMA

GEORGIA

FLORIDA

NEW HAMPSHIRE

VERMONT

MASSACHUSETTS

PENNSYLVANIA

NEW YORK

MAINE

RHODE ISLAND

CONNECTICUT

NEW JERSEY

DELAWARE

MARYLAND

VIRGINIA

NORTH CAROLINA

WEST VIRGINIA

SOUTH CAROLINA

Union states

Confederate states

Slave states that stayed in the Union

Above. The map shows the division of the United States between the Union and the Confederacy, and also indicates the slave states that sided with the Union. But the divisions that led to the Civil War were not only about slavery. They were also about creating a nation where individual freedom and enterprise could flourish.

Right. General Robert E. Lee, the Confederate army commander. He led his troops brilliantly, but was forced to surrender on 9 April 1865.

Above. General Ulysses S. Grant, commander of the Northern army, was elected president in 1868.

Since the United States had become independent from Britain in 1783, the northern and southern states had been gradually drawing apart. The north was a land of small farms and growing industrial cities, whose people held on to the ideal of freedom that had been brought to America with the *Pilgrim Fathers* in the early seventeenth century. In the south, states like Virginia and Georgia depended mainly on cotton, which was grown on large farms by rich landowners using slave labor. But slavery was only one of the causes of the American Civil War which broke out in 1861.

NORTH AND SOUTH Although the United States had been founded in 1790, the truth was that it was two nations: north and south. The north wanted change and progress. The south wanted life to go on as it was. The Constitution signed in 1790 had spoken of justice and liberty. How could this be, people in the north asked, while there were four million slaves in the south?

UNION AND CONFEDERACY By 1850, more than half the American states had banned slavery. In 1860 Abraham Lincoln, who was opposed to slavery, was elected President of the United States. It seemed to the southern states that if they stayed in the Union of states their way of life was doomed. In 1861, 11 southern states broke away and formed their own union, which they called the Confederacy. This was the signal for the outbreak of war with the 23 states of the north.

Was there to be one United States of America, or two groups of states always quarreling with each other? That was the question behind the Civil War. It took four years of bitter fighting to decide. At first, the southern army had better leadership and won several battles. But in July 1863, at Gettysburg in Pennsylvania, the Confederate forces were forced to retreat and this was the turning point of the war. From then on the Union army, led by General Grant, was the more successful force on the battlefield. At last, in April 1865, General

Richmond, Virginia, was the Confederate capital. On 9 April 1865, with northern troops approaching, the people evacuated the city and set fire to it.

Farming and Industry in the USA

Right. Union and Confederate (far right) troops. The Union army had a black troop which the Confederates did not. They were also better armed than their southern opponents.

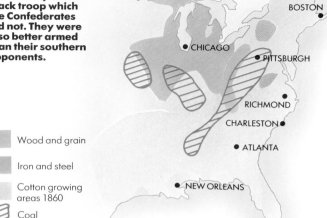

Wood and grain

Iron and steel

Cotton growing areas 1860

Coal

The American Civil War 1861–1865

Right. Before the Civil War, industrial development in the United States was confined almost entirely to the northern states, where essential raw materials such as coal were available.

Left. The major battlefields of the American Civil War.

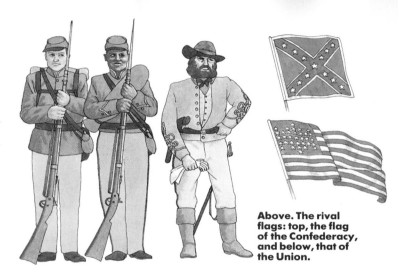

Above. The rival flags: top, the flag of the Confederacy, and below, that of the Union.

Abraham Lincoln 1809–1865

Abraham Lincoln's family lived in a log cabin in Kentucky and were poor farmers. Abraham spent only about a year at school, but he taught himself to read and write. He had several low-paid jobs and then studied to become a lawyer.

By 1847 he had been elected to the House of Representatives and in 1858 he became a senator. Lincoln believed that the division between the northern and southern states would destroy the Union. This was the basis of his presidential campaign in 1861.

After the Civil War, Lincoln pledged himself to "bind up the nation's wounds." But on 14 April 1865 he was shot at the theater. He died the next day.

Lee's Confederate army was forced to surrender.

The war was over, but the cost had been terrible. Over half a million people—about one in 50 people in the USA—had been killed, two-thirds of them by disease caused by the conditions of war. And even after peace had come, bitterness between the north and the south continued for many years.

FREEING THE SLAVES In the middle of the Civil War, President Lincoln signed a proclamation freeing all the slaves in the USA. When the war was over, freedom from slavery and equal rights for all races were written into the United States Constitution. But this did not mean that the troubles of the blacks in the south were over. When the northern troops went home, the south went back to its old ways. Although slavery had been abolished, the blacks in the south still did not have equal rights and it was another 100 years before *discrimination* against them began to break down.

REVOLUTIONS AND EVOLUTION

In Victorian Britain, social classes were clearly distinguished by their clothes.

Islam and *Hinduism*, but they thought of these as *pagan* and inferior.

The Christian churches, both Protestant and Catholic, influenced every aspect of life in Europe. They taught that monarchs, nobles, landowners and employers had been chosen by God to occupy their positions and power. A verse of a hymn sung in English churches put it like this:

The rich man in his castle,
The poor man at his gate,
God made them high or lowly
And ordered their estate.

It was almost impossible to escape from the influence of the churches. They controlled most universities and schools and the entry to most professions. For governments wanting to retain their power, Christian teaching was very convenient. Who had the right to question or criticize rulers who had been chosen by God?

At the beginning of the nineteenth century, when people in the West thought of "civilization" they meant Western civilization, based in Europe and carried by European settlers to areas such as North America. Western thinking was dominated by Christianity and the belief that Genesis, the first book of the Bible, was a complete and literal record of the creation of the world. Europeans knew of other civilizations, such as those of

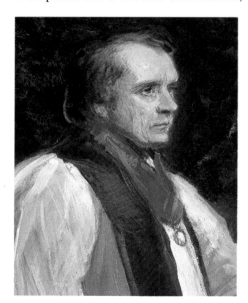

Above. Samuel Wilberforce was the Bishop of Oxford in 1845. He attacked Darwin's views and wanted to see the Church have more power over the everyday life of people.

Right. William Blake's visionary *Book of Job,* one of a series of paintings with Biblical themes that he produced throughout his life. He also wrote, illustrated, printed and published his own poems.

How Ideas Spread

One reason why ideas spread more quickly in the nineteenth century was that steam power made printing much faster and cheaper. The first steam presses were used in 1814 to print *The Times* newspaper in London.

Later printing became even cheaper after new inventions such as machines which set lines of type automatically, and presses which printed on reels of paper instead of separate sheets.

For those who could not read, books and newspapers were read aloud in public. For the first time, ordinary people could hear different views, not just those of their priest.

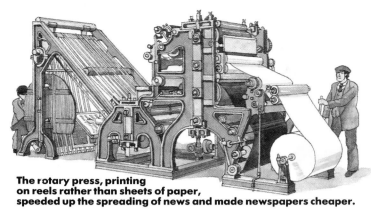

The rotary press, printing
on reels rather than sheets of paper,
speeded up the spreading of news and made newspapers cheaper.

REVOLUTIONARY CHALLENGE The French Revolution
of 1789 had challenged these ideas with its demands for
freedom and equality. On the other side of the Atlantic
Ocean, the same demands had led the American states to
fight for independence from Britain. But European
governments did not want new ideas. They wanted
things to go on as before. Then, in 1859, a book was
published in London that would change the whole way of
thinking in the West.

DARWIN'S BOMBSHELL The book was *The Origin of
Species,* written by Charles Darwin (1809–1882). Darwin
was a British scientist who had traveled widely and
studied the development of plant and animal species.
From his studies, he had worked out the theory of
evolution. This said that the Earth and its plant and
animal life had developed slowly over millions of years
and had not, as many people believed from the Bible,
been created in exactly six days.

Darwin's ideas did not change everyone's way of
thinking at once. But he convinced most scientists—and
scientists, with the improvements they had brought
about in medicine and the standard of living, were very
popular in the nineteenth century. For many years the
churches attacked Darwin fiercely, because he had
produced an explanation of human creation that cast
doubt on the basic ideas behind Western Christian
culture.

THE MELTING POT Darwin's book was just one example
of the way Western ideas were changing. Another
change was the attitude of people towards their rulers.
Almost all countries were ruled by monarchs. But was
this necessary? The United States of America, for
example, managed very well without a monarch and it
gave the people a greater say in how the country was
run.

Other people asked why it was that the poor were
poor. Were they made that way, or had they simply not
had the opportunities and education that the rich had had?

Slowly but surely, in the nineteenth century the ideas
which had previously been the foundation of Western
civilization were going into the melting pot and new ideas
and attitudes were being formed.

Right. Dawes Point,
Sydney, one of the
Beagle's landfalls
on Charles Darwin's
voyage of
discovery.
Below. Darwin in
1840, aged 31, four
years after his
return. He spent the
next 20 years
developing his
theory of
evolution.

The Voyage of the *Beagle*

The *Beagle* set sail
westwards from
Britain in the last
days of 1831. It was
to be a five-year
voyage.

ATLANTIC OCEAN · SEVILLE · ASIA · PACIFIC OCEAN · AFRICA · PHILIPPINES · PACIFIC OCEAN · GALAPAGOS ISLANDS · SOUTH AMERICA · INDIAN OCEAN · BATAVIA · AUSTRALIA · STRAITS OF MAGELLAN · CAPE OF GOOD HOPE · TASMANIA · NEW ZEALAND

The Old World
TIME CHART

	EUROPE	NORTH AND SOUTH AMERICA	REST OF WORLD
AD			
1789	Outbreak of the French Revolution	George Washington becomes the first president of the United States of America	
1792>1815	Napoleonic Wars		
1811>1824		Spain's former colonies in Central and South America achieve independence as separate states, except for the islands of Cuba and Puerto Rico	
1812	French army invades Russia and is defeated outside Moscow		
1815	Congress of Vienna		Britain adds Cape Colony, South Africa, to its empire
1819	First steamship crossing of the Atlantic by the *Savannah*		
1820		Brazil becomes independent from Portugal	
1825	Opening of the Stockton and Darlington Railway in Britain Nicholas I becomes tsar of Russia		
1829			Britain claims the whole of Australia
1830	Revolution in France Revolts in Belgium, Italy and Poland Cholera spreads from Asia to Russia	America's first railway, the South Carolina Railway, opens	
1837	Victoria becomes queen of Britain		
1838			All slaves in the British Empire set free
1839			First British settlers land in New Zealand
1840			New Zealand added to the British Empire
1845>1846	The Great Famine		
1848	Revolution in France Revolts in parts of Italy, Germany and the Austrian Empire *The Communist Manifesto* published The Chartist campaign for democracy in Britain fails		
1849		California Gold Rush	
1854>1856	The Crimean War		
1855	Tsar Nicholas I dies		
1856	Tsar Alexander II takes control		
1857>1858			The Indian Mutiny
1859	*The Origin of Species* published		
1860		Abraham Lincoln becomes president of the USA	
1861>1865		The American Civil War	
1865		Slavery abolished in the USA	

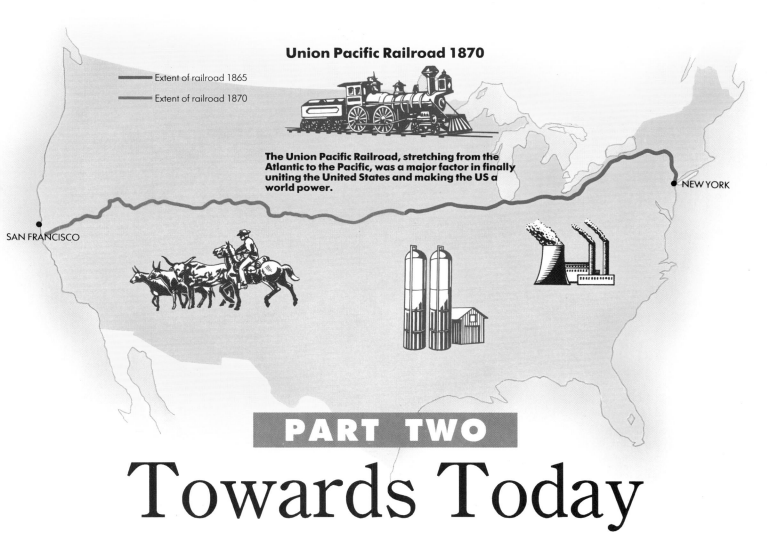

Union Pacific Railroad 1870

— Extent of railroad 1865
— Extent of railroad 1870

The Union Pacific Railroad, stretching from the Atlantic to the Pacific, was a major factor in finally uniting the United States and making the US a world power.

NEW YORK

SAN FRANCISCO

PART TWO
Towards Today

The second half of the nineteenth century saw great changes in the power of different countries, both in Europe—which had played a leading role in political and technological developments for so many centuries—and in the wider world.

FROM THE ATLANTIC TO THE PACIFIC In 1865 in the United States of America, work began on a major engineering project, building a railway linking the Atlantic and Pacific coasts. The Union Pacific Company employed a work force of former Civil War soldiers and Irish *immigrants* to extend its railway line from Omaha, Nebraska in the east, over the Rocky Mountains. Meanwhile, the Chinese laborers of the Central Pacific line set out to meet them from California in the west.

The two lines met at Promontory Point, near the Great Salt Lake in Utah, on 10 May 1869. For the first time, passengers could travel by rail from one side of North America to the other.

GROWTH OF THE USA It was an important moment for the United States, and for the world. The American Civil War (see pages 36–37) was over. The USA was ready to become a major world power. The new railway would

speed up farming development and transport meat and grain from the farms to the cities and ports. It would help Americans to feel that they belonged to one vast country.

Within 20 years the USA had become the world's largest supplier of grain, meat and steel. The country also took the lead in many of the inventions of the second half of the nineteenth century.

Up to now, almost all of America's immigrants had come from Europe. Now, America could look across the Pacific as well as the Atlantic. It stood between the world's two great oceans. In the first half of the nineteenth century, the Atlantic had been the world's great sea highway for passengers and cargoes. In the second half, the Pacific was opened up in the same way.

THE SHRINKING WORLD Meanwhile, faster communications were drawing the rest of the world closer. The late nineteenth century was the age of the steam train and the steamship. In 1872 the French writer Jules Verne published his book *Around the World in Eighty Days*. It was an adventure story, but it contained an important message: faster travel made the world seem smaller and what was happening in the rest of the world was important to everyone.

41

Power Struggles

CHANGING THE MAP OF EUROPE

The map of Europe in the middle of the nineteenth century looked similar in many ways to that of today, with two important differences. Where today's map shows Italy and Germany as two large countries, on the older map there was a mass of small states. Two of the most important changes in Europe between 1851 and 1871 happened when these states were grouped into the two nations of Italy and Germany.

ITALY UNITES The 1848 revolution in Italy (see page 11) was a protest against being ruled by foreign governments. Austria occupied the northern Italian states, the Spanish controlled the southern half of the country and the pope ruled a group of states in the center. The only independent part of Italy was Piedmont, made up of the northwestern state of Piedmont and the island of Sardinia. The 1848 revolution failed to bring any change, but from 1852 onwards Piedmont set out to unite Italy into one nation.

War with Austria in 1859 led to unity between Piedmont and some of its neighbors. In 1860 a rebellion in the south united these to most of the rest of Italy except for the state of Rome, which was controlled by the pope. Finally, in 1870, the pope agreed to hand over all of Rome except for the Vatican City, the small area around St. Peter's Church. At last, after much fighting and bloodshed, Italy was one united country.

The years after Italian unification were disappointing. The very poor southern states were jealous of the prosperity of the north. It seemed to the south that the government's main aim was to make the north even richer.

ONE GERMANY Just as one state, Piedmont, led the unification of Italy, so the largest German state, Prussia, took the lead there. After 1815, Austria ruled about a quarter of what is now Germany. Prussia ruled an area of much the same size. The rest of Germany was made up

The Nation-Builders

Count Camillo Cavour (1810–1861) believed that Italy should be united as a monarchy and not a republic. He was born in Piedmont, which was controlled by Austria. In 1847, he founded a newspaper called *Il Risorgimento* to put forward his views. He became prime minister of Piedmont in 1852 and was able to follow his campaign to drive the Austrians out of northern Italy.

Count Otto von Bismarck (1815–1898) was a Prussian from a wealthy background. After studying, he served as an ambassador for Prussia then became prime minister in 1861. He was determined that Germany should unite under Prussian leadership and go on to become a world power.

Wars with Austria in 1866 and France in 1870 showed Europe the power of the Prussian army, which Bismarck had built up.

Left. Count Camillo Cavour, Sardinian statesman.

Far left. Bismark, in white, at Versailles.

The Unification of Italy 1859–1870

SAVOY
LOMBARDY
TYROL
VENETIA
TRIESTE
PARMA
PIEDMONT
MODENA
FLORENCE
TUSCANY
PAPAL STATES
KINGDOM OF SARDINIA
CORSICA
SARDINIA
KINGDOM OF THE TWO SICILIES

Left. The movement for the unification of Italy began in Piedmont and spread southwards towards the Mediterranean. Venice and Rome were the last states to give way, leaving only Vatican City outside the united Italy.

Kingdom of Sardinia

SCHLESWIG
HOLSTEIN
HANOVER
EAST PRUSSIA
HOLLAND
WESTPHALIA
BERLIN
PRUSSIA
RUSSIAN EMPIRE
BELGIUM
HESSE-NASSAU
SILESIA
BADEN
BAVARIA
PRAGUE
AUSTRIAN EMPIRE
WURTENBURG
SWITZERLAND

The Unification of Germany

Above. Germany, made up of a collection of tiny states, needed unity to combat the large nations that surrounded it. It was this threat that led Prussia to lead the fight for a united Germany.

Prussia 1815

Lands acquired by Prussia to 1867

German Empire 1871

of about 40 small states which were under Austrian control.

In 1866 Prussia defeated Austria after a war that lasted seven weeks. Prussia then took over control of most of the small German states in the north and set up links with the southern states. But the thought of a large united Germany alarmed France, and war between Prussia and France broke out in 1870. The French army was no match for the skilled and well-equipped Prussian troops, however, and by January 1871 France had surrendered.

Now that France was defeated, Prussia could complete its plan for a united Germany. It humiliated France still further by choosing the Palace of Versailles near Paris as the place where Wilhelm I, King of Prussia, was proclaimed *Kaiser* (emperor) of all Germany.

GERMAN STRENGTH Almost at once, Germany became a leading power in western Europe. But French bitterness and shame at its defeat did not fade and Britain also soon became worried by Germany's growing strength. In the last 30 years of the nineteenth century, these tensions increased. They were eventually to spill over in the First World War of 1914 to 1918.

Left. A scene of waste and destruction in the center of Paris during the Prussian siege of the city in 1870–1871. The French were no match for the efficient Prussians and surrendered after 131 days.

Above. On the way to Italian unity, 1860. The revolutionary leader Garibaldi hands over to Victor Emanuel II, King of Sardinia, the land he has conquered in central Italy.

THE WEST COMES TO CHINA

To most Europeans at the start of the nineteenth century, China was a mysterious, unknown country on the other side of the world. For centuries, European traders had been traveling there to buy silk, porcelain and tea. But contacts with Europe had not changed the Chinese. They had their own civilization, which was far older than Europe's. They thought of Westerners as "barbarians."

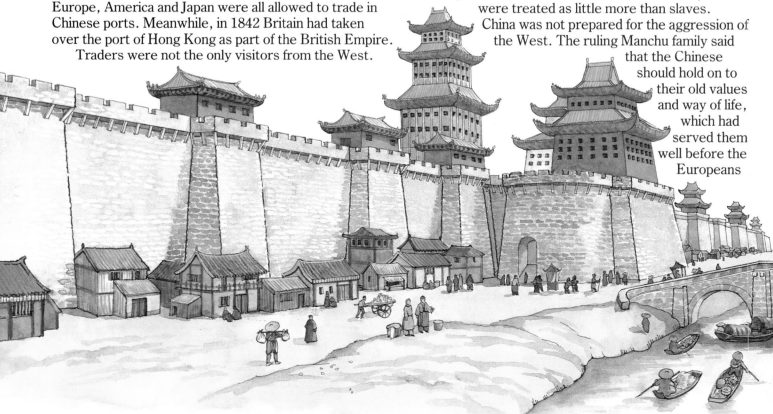

A cartoon from a propaganda book, published in 1891, urging the Chinese to make war on Westerners and resist Western influence. The Chinese resented the fact that many European powers, including Britain, and Russia, had set up trading posts on Chinese territory that were exempted from Chinese law.

THE OPIUM WARS In the eighteenth century, merchants began to bring the drug *opium* into China to pay for Chinese goods. By the 1830s, opium was doing so much harm to Chinese society that the emperor of China ordered European and American traders to stop supplying it. This led to war. In 1839 British forces landed at Chinese ports and threatened to move inland unless the emperor allowed traders to operate freely. He agreed, but war broke out again in 1856. By 1860 Europe, America and Japan were all allowed to trade in Chinese ports. Meanwhile, in 1842 Britain had taken over the port of Hong Kong as part of the British Empire.

Traders were not the only visitors from the West.

Christian *missionaries* also poured into China. They aimed to convert the Chinese *Buddhists*, whom they regarded as *heathen*, to Christianity, whether they wanted to be converted or not. After slavery was abolished in the United States of America (see pages 34–35), the Americans looked to Chinese workers as a source of cheap labor. Thousands were bribed or kidnapped to go to the USA and elsewhere, where they were treated as little more than slaves.

China was not prepared for the aggression of the West. The ruling Manchu family said that the Chinese should hold on to their old values and way of life, which had served them well before the Europeans

The Manchu Family

The Manchu family, or *dynasty*, had ruled China since 1644. They were warriors from Manchuria in the north, who ruled harshly and expanded the Chinese Empire.

The Manchus saw no reason to change the traditional Chinese way of life. China had a huge population, so there seemed no reason to replace cheap manual labor with expensive machines. But the opium traders and missionaries brought Western ideas, one of which was that it was wrong for the wealthy to live in luxury while the peasants often starved to death, an idea that helped to create dissatisfaction.

In 1861 Emperor Hsien Feng died, leaving a son who was still only a child. Hsien Feng's widow, Ci Xi, took over. She put most of her effort into outwitting any ministers who opposed her instead of developing the country. In 1890, for example, she cancelled plans to modernize the navy because she had quarreled with the admirals and spent the money on rebuilding her Summer Palace in Beijing. As a result, Japan defeated China five years later.

Ci Xi lived until 1908, but by then the Manchus had lost power and the scene was set for the revolution four years later.

These women musicians represent Chinese cultural values which were under threat from the West.

arrived. Others argued that China must bring itself up to date with Western inventions such as modern weapons, industries, steamships and railways. If this was done, they said, China would be powerful enough to drive the foreigners out of their land.

YEAR OF REBELLION In the years following the Opium Wars the argument flared up into a series of rebellions. The most serious was the Taiping Rebellion,

China under Foreign Control

Right. Traders of different nationalities had treated China as a kind of treasure-house to be plundered.

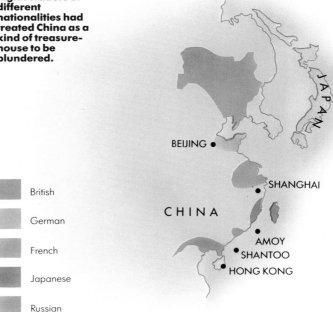

British

German

French

Japanese

Russian

which began in 1850. The Taiping rebels wanted reforms based on Western Christian ideas. For 14 years they fought their way through the most heavily populated part of China, capturing city after city. They were finally defeated by an army led by American and British *mercenaries*.

Several other countries took advantage of China's weakness. Russia took over an area of northern China. France defeated China in a war in 1885, and in 1895 Japan forced China to hand over land and trading rights to them.

THE BOXER RISING A drought in 1899 led to famine. When the government did nothing to help, another rebellion, known as the Boxer Rising, broke out. Its leaders called for the Manchu family to be overthrown and for all foreigners to be "destroyed." At first the rebels were successful, but they were defeated in 1900 by a force of foreign troops.

Although the Boxer Rising failed, it was clear that the Manchu dynasty could no longer govern China properly. Twelve years later it was forced to hand over power to a new government.

The West Gate of Peking, now known as Beijing, China's capital city. The splendor of the imperial city contrasts with the very basic buildings of the farmers on the other side of the river.

45

JAPAN'S LEAP FORWARD

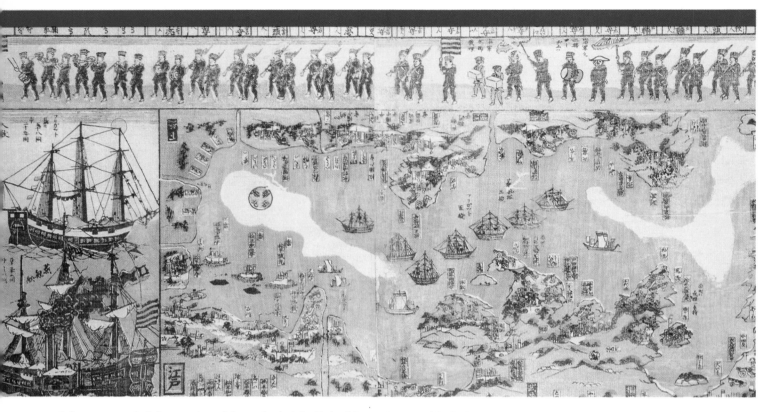

A Japanese artist's impression of the arrival of the United States Navy's "black ships" in 1853.

Japan, like China (see pages 44–45), was another Far Eastern country which was cut off from the rest of the world until the middle of the nineteenth century. It was even more isolated than China. There was no foreign trade, no foreign visitors were allowed to enter the country and no Japanese were allowed to leave.

Japan had an emperor, but the real ruler was the *shogun*, the commander of the army. He controlled the land and the roads and even how the Japanese dressed. His rule was enforced by warriors called *samurai*.

THE BLACK SHIPS Japan's isolation ended suddenly. In July 1853, four United States warships sailed into Tokyo Bay. Two were steamships, and when the Japanese saw black smoke pouring from the funnels they called them "the black ships." The ships brought a message for the emperor: he must open his ports to American ships; if he did not, a larger American force would be sent.

Next year, the Americans were back again, this time with 10 ships and a force of 2,000 men. The emperor was forced to agree to let American trading ships call, and soon Japanese ports were open to ships from all nations.

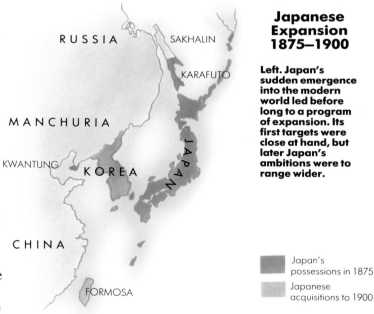

Japanese Expansion 1875–1900

Left. Japan's sudden emergence into the modern world led before long to a program of expansion. Its first targets were close at hand, but later Japan's ambitions were to range wider.

Japan's possessions in 1875

Japanese acquisitions to 1900

THE SHOGUN'S REACTION The emperor's decision upset the shogun, who encouraged the samurai to attack foreigners. When three British men were murdered in

46

Far left. An American visitor takes a pleasure trip round Yokohama.

Left. Traditional Japanese dress in the late nineteenth century: a farm worker and a lady of fashion.

Below. *The Great Wave of Kanagawa* by the Japanese artist Katsushika Hokusai, who died in 1849. His work influenced many late nineteenth-century European painters.

1862 and the shogun refused to punish the murderers, British ships attacked the city of Kagoshima. In 1863 a Japanese force fired on Dutch, French and American merchant ships and a fleet of 16 warships was sent to destroy it. The message was clear: Western nations were not going to let the shogun interfere with trade.

The shogun had feared that contact with the West would make the Japanese want more freedom and prosperity for themselves, and he was right. In 1865 civil war broke out and after three years' fighting the shogun was defeated.

The New Japan

1853 Arrival of the US 'black ships'
1854 Trading treaty signed with the USA
1865 Civil war between traditionalists and reformers
1867 Emperor Komei succeeded by his son Mutsuhito who introduced *Meiji* ("Enlightened Peace") government".
1872 Introduction of Western-style education, policing, justice and banking. Japan's first railway opened
1889 Parliamentary government introduced, but the emperor had the right to reverse its decisions

MODERNIZING JAPAN From then on, the Japanese attitude to the West suddenly changed. British engineers were invited to build Japan's first railway, which opened in 1872. The ban on Japanese travel abroad was lifted, and British and American advisers were brought in to help to organize post and telegraph services.

In 1871 a group of learned Japanese men was sent abroad to learn about Western civilization. They were away for nearly two years, visiting the United States and Europe. They studied everything in great detail and when they returned they were full of news about what they had seen, from cameras to steam engines and from schools to post offices.

Japan at once started a program of modernization which was to continue over the next 60 years. Its aim was to make Japan a world power that was respected by other nations. But it was not long before the new, more confident Japan began to look dangerous. In 1894 it launched its first modern foreign war, against the Chinese in Korea. Ten years after that, the new Japanese navy was strong enough to sink or capture the entire Russian fleet in the Russo-Japanese War.

The New Colonies

SOUTH AFRICA AND THE BOERS

With so many European countries building up their empires overseas during the nineteenth century, their interests sometimes clashed. One place where this happened was in South Africa—with tragic results.

RIVALS FOR THE CAPE The Dutch had first settled at the Cape of Good Hope in 1650, mainly to provide a harbor for Dutch ships on their way to and from the East Indies. But some Dutch settlers went inland and started farming. They became known as *Boers*, from the Dutch word for "farmer."

After the Congress of Vienna in 1815 (see page 7) the Cape became a British colony. Britain wanted it for the same reason as the Dutch, to use it as a staging post for ships going to the East. British settlers began to arrive at the Cape; soon there were 4,000 of them and it was decided that the language of the area should be English. This was bad enough for the Dutch settlers, but there was worse to come. In 1838 slavery was banned throughout the British Empire and the Dutch were ordered to free their slaves.

THE GREAT TREK Many Boers strongly disliked being ruled by Britain and decided to travel north to areas beyond British control. This movement north, called the Great Trek, began in 1834 and went on until 1839. About 14,000 Boers took part. The land they reached was occupied by the Zulu and Matabele tribes. The Boers, with their better

Southern Africa 1800–1900

TRANSVAAL

ORANGE FREE STATE

ULUNDI

ISWANDHLWANA

NATAL

DURBAN

CAPE COLONY

CAPE TOWN

⚔ Battles of the Zulu War

← Great Trek 1840

▮ Boer States

▮ Area of conflict during Boer War

Above. This map shows how both the British and the Boers steadily moved northwards to take over increasing tracts of the tribal lands of South Africa.

The battle of Spion Kop in Natal in January 1900. It was a Boer victory which humiliated the British forces.

The Zulu

The Zulu were the most powerful of the original tribes of southern Africa. In 1810 they chose a new chief, Shaka, who organized the tribe as a conquering army. He introduced the *assegai*, a spear designed for stabbing rather than throwing, and larger shields for extra protection. The Zulu drove back rival tribes and gained control of a large area of eastern South Africa. Shaka was murdered in 1828, but the Zulu conquests continued until they were checked by the Boers 10 years later.

The Zulu had lost land to the Boers and to the British, and there was a new border dispute in 1877. In 1879 the British ordered Chief Cetawayo to disband his troops. When he refused, the British invaded Zululand.

The first British attack was beaten off, but six months later a stronger force invaded and defeated the Zulus. In 1887 the British took direct control of Zululand and 10 years later it became the British colony of Natal. However, Zulu defiance of British rule continued into the twentieth century.

European weapons, drove the tribes back and cleared the country for themselves. By 1856 they had set up two independent Boer republics, Orange Free State and Transvaal.

DIAMONDS AND GOLD The Boers and the British lived alongside each other uneasily until, in 1867, diamonds were discovered on the western border of Orange Free State. This changed the whole future of South Africa, as a poor farming country became a rich supplier of precious stones and metals. The British claimed the territory where the discoveries were made and this was resented by the Boers.

Meanwhile the British were finding it more and more difficult to govern South Africa. Things became worse in 1884 when gold was discovered at what is now

Johannesburg in the Transvaal. This turned out to be the biggest goldfield in the world and soon there was a "gold rush" like the one in 1849 in California (see page 33). Prospectors rushed to the Transvaal from all over the world, and once again the Boers felt that they had been cheated of what should have been theirs.

THE BOER WAR By the 1890s the tensions between the Boers and the British had reached boiling point. The British had only a small army in South Africa, but they declared war in October 1899, expecting an easy victory. They were wrong. The Boers fought hard and it took a large army sent from Britain to defeat them. The result was that the Boer republics became part of the Union of South Africa, and remained within the British Empire for the next 60 years.

A Boer farmstead. When they settled in the Orange Free State and Transvaal, the Boers showed much of the same spirit as the American pioneers.

THE SCRAMBLE FOR AFRICA

The African Explorers

David **Livingstone** (1813–1873), a Scottish doctor and missionary, first went to Africa in 1840 to set up a mission in what is now Botswana. In 1849 he and a hunter called William Oswell crossed the Kalahari Desert, and over the next few years he explored the Zambesi River, discovering the great waterfalls which he named after Queen Victoria. His last exploration in 1866 was to search for the sources of the Congo and Nile rivers. He died of fever on 1 May 1873.

Sir Henry Morton Stanley (1841–1904) was a Welsh-born journalist who went to Africa in 1869 to find Livingstone, missing for three years. They met on the shores of Lake Tanganyika in 1871. After Livingstone's death, Stanley led two explorations of the area round the River Congo.

Sir Richard Burton (1821–1890) began his exploration of Somalia in East Africa in 1854. Later, with a fellow army officer called John Hanning Speke, he led an expedition through Tanzania to find the source of the Nile.

Heinrich Barth (1821–1865), born in Hamburg in Germany made his first journey in 1845 across North Africa and into Syria. He spent nearly six years in Africa, exploring the northern part of what is now Nigeria.

In 1800, Europe knew very little about Africa apart from the Cape area in the south. Sailors knew the Mediterranean shore and a few trading posts around the east and west coasts. The rest of Africa was a mystery. On the map, it was shown as a great white space.

Yet by 1914 Africa had become a patchwork of colonies. The British, French, Germans, Spanish, Portuguese, Italians and Belgians had carved it up between them.

THE GREAT EXPLORERS It was explorers, not invading European troops, who "opened up" Africa to European influence. Heinrich Barth of Germany crossed the Sahara Desert from north to south in about 1850. At about the same time David Livingstone, a Scottish missionary, explored the Zambesi River in East Africa. Other explorers traced the course of the River Nile northwards and the Congo River westwards.

Although Europeans were excited to read about

The Suez Canal

The idea of a canal linking the Mediterranean and the Red Sea is as old as the ancient Egyptians. The canal, 96 miles long, took 10 years to build and was opened in 1869. It was designed by French engineers and built with French and Egyptian money. In 1875 Britain bought the Egyptian share, forging a link with Egypt which lasted until 1955.

Colonial Africa 1870

The European powers quite cold-bloodedly carved up Africa between them, with no thought of the interests of the native populations. By 1914 almost the entire continent was controlled from Europe.

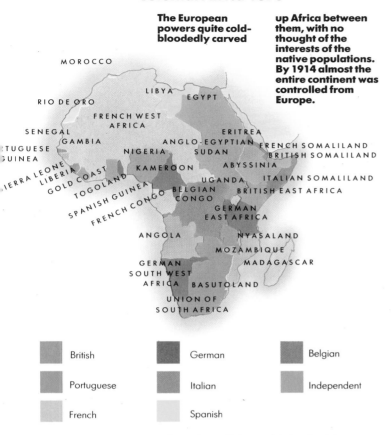

British	German	Belgian
Portuguese	Italian	Independent
French	Spanish	

the European trading nations, especially Britain. To safeguard ships passing through the Canal, Britain took over the "protection" of Egypt and later gained control of the Sudan. Britain, France and Italy all had colonies at the southern end of the Red Sea. Trade with East Africa could now go through ports in these colonies instead of taking the long way around by the Cape.

SPHERES OF INFLUENCE The second reason for the scramble for Africa was the result of the Franco-Prussian War of 1870–1871 (see page 43). France, which was defeated, looked for an empire to restore its position as a world power. Germany, which was victorious, needed new markets for its industries and colonies for its growing population. In a series of treaties beginning in 1885, European countries agreed among themselves on their "spheres of influence," the parts of Africa they would take control of, regardless of the feelings of the Africans. The boundaries between European colonies often split up tribal lands or brought together tribes which had been enemies for hundreds of years.

Some Europeans treated the Africans better than others did. In the Belgian Congo (present-day Zaïre), local workers were little more than slaves. In the British and German colonies, either the government or the missionaries did set up schools and provide medical care for the local people. But Europeans were interested in Africa mainly for their own benefit. Many goods that were valuable in Europe—such as precious metals and stones, minerals like copper and nickel, tropical hardwoods and farm produce—were shipped there from Africa, and in return the African colonies provided markets for European manufactured goods. By 1914 only two small areas of Africa, the state of Liberia (set up in 1847 by freed American slaves) and the kingdom of Abyssinia (present-day Ethiopia), were not part of a European empire or under European "protection."

these adventures, at first they did not think of taking over the newly mapped areas. The scramble for Africa did not begin until about 1870. There were two reasons for this.

THE SUEZ CANAL One was the opening of the Suez Canal in 1869. As it linked the Mediterranean with the Red Sea, it shortened shipping routes to India and the Far East by several thousand miles. It became vital to

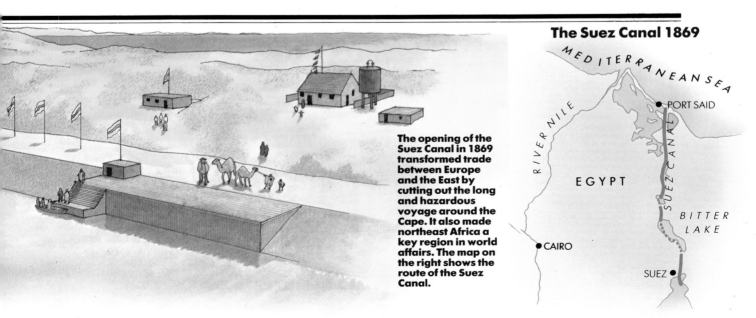

The Suez Canal 1869

The opening of the Suez Canal in 1869 transformed trade between Europe and the East by cutting out the long and hazardous voyage around the Cape. It also made northeast Africa a key region in world affairs. The map on the right shows the route of the Suez Canal.

AUSTRALIA AND NEW ZEALAND

Australia and New Zealand were the last areas of the world to be added to the British Empire by white settlers, but once settlement began it grew very rapidly.

The new Australians settled around the coast. The *outback*—the inland desert—was populated by a small number of Aboriginals, the native people of Australia. No European had crossed the outback until 1861, when the explorers Burke and Wills died on their return journey.

Settlers who went to New Zealand found a climate that was similar to that of Britain and they were able to adapt to their new country more easily.

SHEEP AND GOLD Australian settlers in New South Wales found land that was perfect for grazing sheep, and wool became the foundation of Australia's prosperity. By 1850 the country was the largest producer of wool in the world.

Then, in 1851, large deposits of gold were found in New South Wales and Victoria. Later, more was found in Queensland, together with coal, zinc and other minerals. Australia was now able to add industry to its activities and more settlers from Britain arrived to share in its wealth. By the 1890s Australia's two main cities, Sydney and Melbourne, each had populations of nearly half a million.

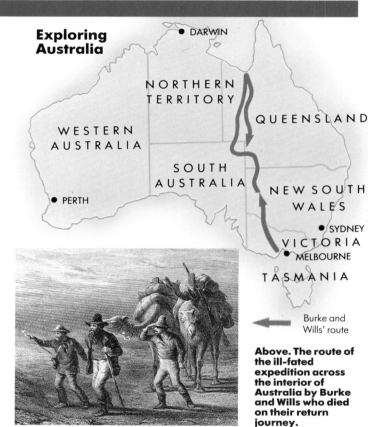

Exploring Australia

DARWIN

NORTHERN TERRITORY

WESTERN AUSTRALIA

PERTH

SOUTH AUSTRALIA

QUEENSLAND

NEW SOUTH WALES

SYDNEY

VICTORIA

MELBOURNE

TASMANIA

Burke and Wills' route

Above. The route of the ill-fated expedition across the interior of Australia by Burke and Wills who died on their return journey.

Left. In 1851, gold was found at Ballarat and Bendigo in Victoria, creating a furious gold rush of men sure they would find a fortune.

Above. The Burke and Wills expedition setting out on their ill-fated journey across Australia from Cooper Creek in 1861.

Below. Aboriginal spears and boomerangs were no defense against the settlers' guns.

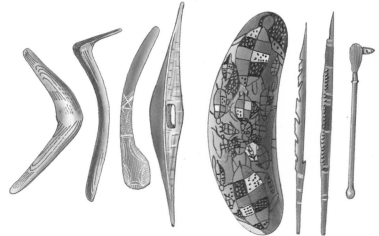

GOVERNOR DAVEY'S
PROCLAMATION
TO THE ABORIGINES
1816.

"Why Massa Guberner", said Black Jack... "Yon Proclamation all gammon"
"Him blackfellow read him eh? He no learn him read book."
"Read that then" said the Governor, pointing to a picture.

Above. A savage contemporary comment on the "civilized" British attitude toward the aboriginals.

Colonization of New Zealand

Above. Maori weapons of war reflect their preference for hand-to-hand fighting. They used short hand spears, top, and clubs, above.

Above. White settlements in New Zealand began in the North Island in 1830. They expanded southwards as coal and gold were found and more farming land was opened up.

Left. Maori chief Hone Heke Pokai. The Maoris lived mainly in the North Island of New Zealand. They were tough, intelligent and industrious and they were trained warriors. They lived in villages and farmed the surrounding areas.

THE FATE OF THE ABORIGINALS The bad side of the story of white settlement in Australia concerns the treatment of the Aboriginals. There were about 300,000 Aboriginals in Australia when the Europeans arrived. They lived by *hunting and gathering*, in the same way as their ancestors had done for many thousands of years. When the white settlers arrived with their guns, the Aboriginals could do little to resist them. Thousands were killed, many of them simply hunted down for sport. Although Australians prided themselves on their democracy, it was halfway through the twentieth century before the Aboriginals were given any civil rights at all.

MAORI WARS The native people of New Zealand, the Maori, were at first treated no better by the white settlers. Britain claimed New Zealand as part of its empire in 1840, when there were about 2,000 whites living there. During the next 20 years this number grew to 100,000 and by the 1880s it had reached half a million. Britain bought South Island from the Maori, but promised that whites would not settle on their land in North Island. This promise was broken and the result was 10 years of fighting between 1861 and 1871, during which 2000 Maori were killed.

NEW ZEALAND'S WEALTH New Zealand was a poor, struggling country, despite the discovery of gold in the 1850s, until the invention of the refrigerated ship. This made all the difference to New Zealand farmers. There was more profit in mutton and lamb than in wool, and New Zealand became a major supplier of cheap meat to Britain. Soon, a large dairy industry was built up after it was found that New Zealand butter could be sold in Britain more cheaply than British butter, despite the cost of shipping it there.

THE AMERICAN BOOM

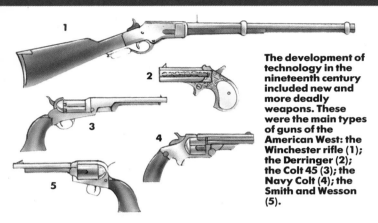

The development of technology in the nineteenth century included new and more deadly weapons. These were the main types of guns of the American West: the Winchester rifle (1); the Derringer (2); the Colt 45 (3); the Navy Colt (4); the Smith and Wesson (5).

The end of the American Civil War in 1865 (see pages 36–37) was a landmark in the history of the United States. It marked a new start in the development of the farming land of the Midwest and in the buildup of American industry.

GUNS AND BARBED WIRE The great cattle-ranching states lay in a belt stretching from Montana and North Dakota in the north to Texas in the south. In the early days, cattle had been allowed to roam freely and were rounded up twice a year. In 1874 came the invention of barbed wire, which provided a cheap means for ranchers to fence in their cattle. The inventor's factory was soon making 600 miles of the wire a day. But its use also meant the end of the pioneer days when a settler could claim a plot of land and farm it for himself. Now, the big farmers—the "cattle kings"—saw off new settlers with guns.

GROWING INDUSTRY The amount of steel made in the United States in 1895 was 300 times greater than it had been in 1867. This gives an idea of the rapid growth of industry during those years. America had its own rich resources of coal and metal ores. It had its own vast market for manufactured goods. Many of the new inventions that were to shape modern life, such as the sewing machine, the typewriter, the telephone and the electric light bulb, were American.

United States industry was the first to develop "big

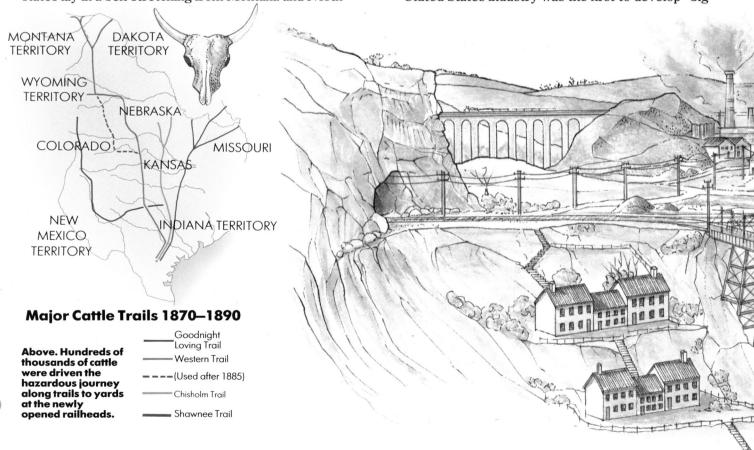

Major Cattle Trails 1870–1890

Above. Hundreds of thousands of cattle were driven the hazardous journey along trails to yards at the newly opened railheads.

—— Goodnight Loving Trail
—— Western Trail
- - - - (Used after 1885)
—— Chisholm Trail
—— Shawnee Trail

US Overseas Interests c.1900

US overseas interests

Above. From 1867, the United States built up its influence in the Pacific. The linking of the Pacific and Atlantic Oceans by the Panama Canal in 1914 opened up the eastern US ports to Pacific trade. Until 1979, the United States controlled the canal and surrounding land.

multimillionaire who dominated the US steel industry. Philip Armour, who started his working life on his father's farm, became head of a company which controlled the meat-packing industry. Other millionaires made their money from railways, oil and the telegraph service. These industrial leaders were often called the "robber barons" because of the methods they used to increase their profits.

LOOKING WESTWARD The opening of the Union Pacific Railroad across the United States in 1869 (see pages 14–15) led Americans to think of the markets waiting for their goods across the Pacific Ocean in Asia. They had already forced China and Japan to open their ports to American ships (see pages 44–45 and 46–47). The United States now set about establishing shipping routes across the Pacific, together with a chain of naval bases to protect them. The first of these bases, set up in 1867, was on Midway Island. Over the next 30 years, the map of the Pacific became dotted with US bases.

While European countries split up Africa into "spheres of influence" (see pages 50–51), the USA built up its own. It bought Alaska from Russia in 1867. War with Spain in 1898 brought it three former Spanish possessions: Puerto Rico in the Caribbean, and the Philippines and Guam in the Pacific. Hawaii became a United States possession in the same year. Almost unnoticed by the rest of the world, the USA had become a world power.

business" methods. Businesspeople built up large groups of companies in order to control wages and selling prices in whole industries. A Scotsman called Andrew Carnegie who had come to America as a poor boy became a

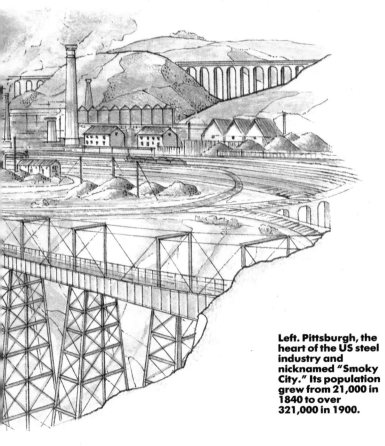

Left. Pittsburgh, the heart of the US steel industry and nicknamed "Smoky City." Its population grew from 21,000 in 1840 to over 321,000 in 1900.

Above. A Cheyenne painting on skin depicting Custer's Last Stand in 1876. Colonel George Armstrong Custer was campaigning against the Sioux Indians led by Sitting Bull. He discovered an Indian encampment near the Little Big Horn river and attacked it against orders. His 264-strong cavalry was outnumbered ten to one and Custer and every one of his men were killed.

GIVE ME YOUR POOR . . .

Immigration into the US

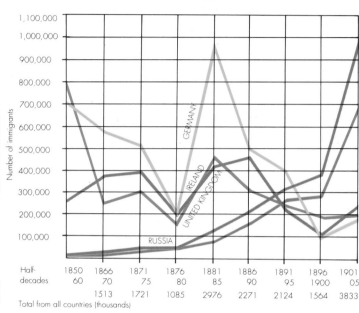

Half-decades	1850 60	1866 70	1871 75	1876 80	1881 85	1886 90	1891 95	1896 1900	1901 05
Total from all countries (thousands)		1513	1721	1085	2976	2271	2124	1564	3833

The growth of the United States of America would not have been possible without the millions of immigrants who poured into the country. In the 1870s there were nearly three million of them; in the 1880s more than five million entered the country. Immigration reached a peak in the first 10 years after 1900, when almost nine million people arrived.

THE "NEW" IMMIGRANTS Before 1865, most immigrants to the USA had come from Britain, Ireland and Germany. Slowly, towards the end of the century, the numbers arriving from these countries fell and were replaced by increasing numbers from Italy and Russia. The Italians were fleeing from the poverty of the south of Italy after unification (see p. 42). The Russians were also escaping from poverty. Many Jews from Russia and eastern Europe had a more urgent reason for leaving for America—they were being persecuted and even

Above. Earlier migrants to the US had come mainly from northern and western Europe. Later, more arrived from southern and eastern Europe.

Above left: Immigrants to the USA leave Ellis Island after medical checks to begin their new lives.

Left. For many, the journey had begun in eastern Europe, from where they had been forced to flee for their lives.

The New Americans

Changes in Europe were reflected in the pattern of migration to the USA after the end of the American Civil War. German, British and Irish migrants were in the majority until the 1890s. But as German and British industry grew and developed, more jobs became available to the work force in those countries, and fewer people needed to emigrate to find jobs in order to feed their families. Russians and Italians then began to migrate in huge numbers. Many of the Russian emigrants were Jews, driven into exile by persecution in their own country. Italians were reacting against the dashing of their hopes of a more prosperous future at home after the unification of Italy.

56

Immigrants had to take whatever work they could get, for the lowest pay. Many worked in the clothing trade, in cramped conditions known as "sweat shops."

US Population Density 1890

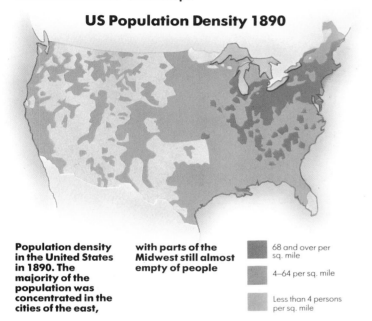

Population density in the United States in 1890. The majority of the population was concentrated in the cities of the east,

with parts of the Midwest still almost empty of people

68 and over per sq. mile

4–64 per sq. mile

Less than 4 persons per sq. mile

The Statue of Liberty

After 1886, the first sight that immigrants sailing into New York Harbor had of the United States of America was the Statue of Liberty. Rising more than 100 feet above the water, the statue carries a torch representing liberty in her right hand and a book of laws in her left. On the base a poem specially written for the Statue of Liberty begins:

Give me your tired, your poor, Your huddled masses yearning to breathe free . . .

It was created by the French sculptor F. Bartholdi and was a gift from the French to the American people, commemorating the alliance of France and the USA during the American War of Independence and marking its centenary.

murdered at home. Poles, Czechs, Hungarians, Romanians, Bulgarians, Greeks and Scandinavians all swelled the numbers of immigrants. The millions arriving across the Atlantic Ocean were joined by Chinese who came across the Pacific to California until 1882, when further Chinese immigration was banned.

THE "NEW" COUNTRY Not everyone was allowed to stay. Immigrants from Europe were first taken to Ellis Island in New York Harbor and given medical checks. If they were unfit, they were sent back home. If they passed the tests, they were allowed in and could go where they wanted.

The United States needed the immigrants, but it wanted them to be proud of their new country. The mixture of races and cultures presented a problem. To become full US citizens the immigrants had to learn English. They were expected to honor the United States flag, the Stars and Stripes, and every school day began with a salute to the flag.

Few of the new immigrants had any money, so they headed for the industrial cities. There, they found work

in Chicago's meat factories, the steel mills of Pittsburgh and the textile mills of Philadelphia. Many Italians, Irish and Jews stayed in New York, where they worked long hours for poor pay in industries like clothing manufacture.

Ethnic groups tended to stay together, enjoying the language, culture, religion and cooking they were used to. To save money, they packed their houses with people, causing the problem of overcrowding. The immigrant areas of many American cities quickly became slums. Life for poor immigrants was tough—but not as tough as it would have been if they had stayed at home.

LAND OF OPPORTUNITY America was more a land of hard work than of opportunity for the new immigrants, but their children found the opportunities. They had been born American citizens, and they had no memories of "the old country" to regret. They had been educated in American schools and had come to accept the American way of life. These second-generation immigrants became absorbed into American culture and proved that, as one writer has said, America was *the great melting pot where all races of Europe are melting and re-forming.*

THE OTHER AMERICA

The pampas, or grasslands, of South America were ideal grazing grounds for cattle, and Argentina, in particular, became a leading supplier of meat to Europe.

The United States of America became a world power by using the strength of a large country whose people, after the American Civil War (see pp. 36–37), mostly forgot their arguments and worked together. It might seem strange that the 10 countries of South America did not do the same, once they had become independent in the 1820s. But there were a number of reasons why.

GENERALS AND STRONG MEN One reason was that each country was ruled by a government, usually headed by a general, which enjoyed power and did not want to give it up to a United States of South America. Another was that Spain and Portugal, which had controlled South America for three centuries before independence, had not invested any money there. They had simply taken what they wanted and put nothing back.

A third reason was South America's geography. The Andes Mountains runs down its western side, leaving a thin Pacific coastal strip which was almost entirely cut off from the rest of the continent. On the east, in Brazil, the great tropical rain forest of the Amazon stretches for thousands of kilometers. North of this is a high plateau where South American Indians—whose ancestors had been conquered by the Europeans in the sixteenth century—made a poor living from peasant farming.

The tropical forests, too, were rich in resources. Here, a rubber tree is tapped in a Brazilian forest.

In the interior, away from the cities, there was little real government. A local strong man, called a *caudillo*, would collect a gang around him and take over an area, controlling the small farmers through fear. Some *caudillos* built up armies large enough to start wars and rebellions, and for most of the nineteenth century fighting was going on in one part of South America or another.

Two Strong Men

Francisco Lopez (1827–1870) succeeded his father as president of Paraguay in 1862. At 18 he had been made commander-in-chief of the Paraguayan army and he had come to believe that any problem could be solved by military force. As soon as Lopez became president he built up a huge Paraguayan army — the largest in South America — and set out to pursue his dream of conquering the continent. He declared war on Argentina, Brazil and Uruguay, but his plans ended in disaster. The Paraguayans suffered defeat after defeat, and Lopez himself was killed in battle in 1870. He left his country impoverished and half its population dead.

Dom Pedro II of Brazil (1825–1891), by contrast, was a ruler who devoted his attention to modernizing his country. He became emperor of Brazil in 1831, when he was five, but he was 14 before he obtained real power.

Below. General Francisco Lopez, President of Paraguay from 1862 to 1870.

Dom Pedro was determined to develop Brazil's trade and industry and so improve the lives of his people. He introduced a European-style banking system and encouraged the development of the coffee and rubber industries. He took an interest in new inventions, such as photography and the telephone, and supported the building of Brazil's first railway and the first submarine telegraph link between South America and Europe. But Brazil's rich farmers still relied on slave labor and when slavery was abolished in 1888 they forced Dom Pedro to abdicate as emperor.

1 One of the results of the new interest in science was the start of the chemical industry. The first synthetic dye was made in 1856 by William Perkin when he was only 18 years old. By the 1870s Germany was in the lead in this field. Other new products included linoleum (1860), the first cheap mass-produced floor-covering.

2 Joseph Lister, a British surgeon introduced antiseptics to the medical world. They reduced the risk of infection and many people survived operations which before would have killed them. They were in widespread use by the 1880s.

3 Experiments with flight were in progress at this time. Otto Lilienthal was building and flying gliders in Germany in the 1890s.

South American States 1888

VENEZUELA
BRITISH
DUTCH
FRENCH
COLOMBIA
GUIANA
ECUADOR
PERU
BRAZIL
BOLIVIA
PACIFIC OCEAN
ATLANTIC OCEAN
URUGUAY
CHILE
ARGENTINA

South America in 1888, showing the major political divisions across the continent.

Right. South American culture extended back thousands of years before the Europeans.

THE LAST SLAVES IN AMERICA Some landowners built up large estates where they grew sugar or coffee. In Brazil, many of these estates were worked by slave labor until 1888, when slavery was at last banned. Brazilian landowners faced ruin, but they were saved by the new demand for rubber, which grew easily in the tropical climate and did not need a large force of workers.

Elsewhere in South America, other new demands created new wealth. Improved methods of canning led to the development of the corned beef industry, using cattle reared on the *pampas*, or grasslands, which were similar to the North American prairies. Tropical hardwood trees were in demand for furniture and a timber industry grew up on the edges of the rain forests. Phosphates and nitrates were mined and exported as fertilizers.

DIVIDED CONTINENT There was no Industrial Revolution in South America. This was partly because of the lack of coal and iron ore, but mainly because no-one wanted to invest money to start industries. Although the 10 South American nations were independent, they still behaved like colonies. They survived by exporting raw materials to North America and Europe in exchange for manufactured goods. The USA was also happy that South America remained divided and did not become a rival power.

Making the Modern World
THE INDUSTRIAL RACE

On 1 May 1851, more than 30,000 people gathered in a huge new iron and glass building in Hyde Park, London. They had come to see Queen Victoria open the Great Exhibition.

"BRITISH IS BEST" The Great Exhibition included products from all over the world, but pride of place was given to the products of British industry and the British Empire. The exhibition attracted over six million visitors from all over Britain and across the world. The organizers wanted all of them to take home the message that "British is best."

In 1851, this was true. Britain's Industrial Revolution had been the first in the world and Britain was still the most important manufacturing country. Its empire was the world's largest and was still growing. Most British people expected things to go on getting better and better.

THE USA CATCHES UP Although Britain did not realize it at first, the industrial world was changing. One of the first signs was another exhibition which was held in Philadelphia, Pennsylvania in 1876 to celebrate 100 years of American independence. This showed how quickly the United States of America had developed since the end of the Civil War in 1865 (see pages 36–37). All the products of America's new industries were on display, together with new American inventions.

One of these new inventions was the telephone, which had been invented that year by Alexander Graham Bell, a Scotsman who had emigrated to the United States to make his fortune. This, combined with later American

The Eiffel Tower, built as the centerpiece of the Paris Exhibition in 1889.

inventions such as the *phonograph*, photographic film and machines for setting printers' type automatically, made the USA the world leader in communications. Americans were the first to make manufactured goods from *mass-produced* parts which were fitted together on a *production line*. By the 1870s many products were made in this way, which took less time and so cost less. America later dominated world industry with such mass-produced products as sewing machines, typewriters, cameras and, in the twentieth century, cars.

In the nineteenth century, steel was an essential part of the machines that manufactured goods and of many goods themselves. By 1890 the USA had overtaken Britain as the world's largest producer of steel. Ten years later it was producing more steel than the other leading countries, Britain and Germany, put together.

GERMANY JOINS THE RACE Germany, the third runner in the industrial race, had won second place in steel production by 1890. German scientists and engineers had also been busy. Their achievements included important improvements in *chemical dyes* and the invention of two kinds of *internal combustion engine*—gasoline-driven and diesel. The British were still inventive too, but they were more concerned with improving existing machines and methods than with developing new ones. For a while, their huge empire protected their industry from trading rivals, but after about 1880 it was no longer true that Britain was "the workshop of the world."

Right. Alexander Graham Bell's first telephone receiver, produced in 1875 under stiff competition from other inventors.

Left. Isaac Singer's 1851 sewing machine. This was to transform the clothing industry, which could make garments cheaper and quicker.

Thomas Alva Edison with the first sound recording machine, the phonograph — one of his many inventions. Largely self-taught, Edison set up his first laboratory at the age of 10. He took out more than 1,000 patents during his career.

Right. The Gatling Gun, 1863, which was first used with devastating effect in the American Civil War.

Left. George Eastman's plastic roll film, 1884, marked the beginning of photography as a popular pastime.

Some American Inventions

1851 Singer sewing machine. Isaac Singer's was not the first sewing machine, but it was a great improvement on earlier models and was the first to be mass-produced for the home.

1869 Celluloid. This was the first plastic material, useful but dangerous as it was highly flammable.

1876 Telephone. Invented by Alexander Graham Bell, a Scotsman who had settled in the USA.

1882 Electric light bulb. Invented by Thomas Alva Edison as a cheaper and better alternative to gas lighting.

1884 Camera film. Invented by George Eastman. Previously, photographers had used cumbersome glass plates.

1886 Linotype. This automatic typesetting machine, which set a line of type at a time, was invented by Ottmar Mergenthaler, a German watch-maker who had emigrated to the USA.

1886 Phonograph (early record player). Another of Thomas Alva Edison's inventions, this was the first sound system, recording sound on a tinfoil cylinder.

1889 Movie camera. Eastman's invention of camera film led Edison to develop a camera to take moving pictures, which could be watched through a hand-held viewer.

Steel Production 1895

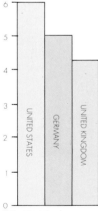

UNITED STATES — 6
GERMANY — 5
UNITED KINGDOM — 4.2
Million Metric Tonnes

Left. A significant year for British industry was 1895, when Germany's steel production overtook Britain's for the first time. Before that, Britain had maintained her lead in the production race, which had been gained by being the first nation to embark on the Industrial Revolution and introduce new machinery and practices.

Exhibition 1851

Full title: The Great Exhibition of the Works and Industry of All Nations
Planning began: 1849
Building began: 30 July 1850
Exhibition open: 1 May–15 October 1851
Exhibitors: 13,937
Visitors: 6,039,205
The Great Exhibition was held in the Crystal Palace on the south side of Hyde Park in London, opposite where the Albert Hall now stands. After the Exhibition, the Crystal Palace was rebuilt at Sydenham in south London. It was destroyed by fire in November 1936.

THE STEAMSHIP AGE

From the beginning of history until the nineteenth century, ships were powered by the wind or by men using oars. If there was no wind a ship would be unable to move, sometimes for days. If there was a storm, the sails could be torn down and the ship could be lost.

THE FIRST STEAMSHIPS Soon after the steam engine was invented in the late eighteenth century, there were several attempts to build steam-powered ships. At first, these were paddle wheelers which were used on canals and rivers and for short voyages between coastal ports. The first steamship to cross the Atlantic Ocean was the *Savannah* in 1819. It had both engines and sails and it traveled most of the way using wind power.

The engines in the early steamships were inefficient and used huge amounts of fuel. But this improved when shipbuilders began to use propellers instead of paddles, and to fit more efficient engines, until by the 1860s the steamships could compete with sailing ships. They could also be larger than sailing ships,

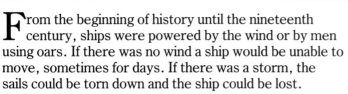

Mark Twain, author of *The Adventures of Tom Sawyer* and *The Adventures of Huckleberry Finn*, spent about 15 years as a pilot of paddle wheelers on the Mississippi river. His real name was Samuel Langhorne Clemens. His pseudonym is a boatman's phrase meaning a depth of water of two fathoms.

as their hulls, or basic frames, were made of iron or steel instead of wood.

The Great Race

In 1838 two groups of businessmen competed for the British government's contract to carry mail across the Atlantic by steamship. They organized a race between the *Sirius* and the *Great Western*.

The *Sirius* ran out of fuel but the crew kept the engine going by burning furniture and it became the first ship to cross the Atlantic using steam power alone. The *Great Western* completed the trip in 15 days, three days faster than the *Sirius*, and still had coal left.

But to the fury of both groups the British government gave the contract to the Canadian Samuel Cunard. His Cunard Line still operates today.

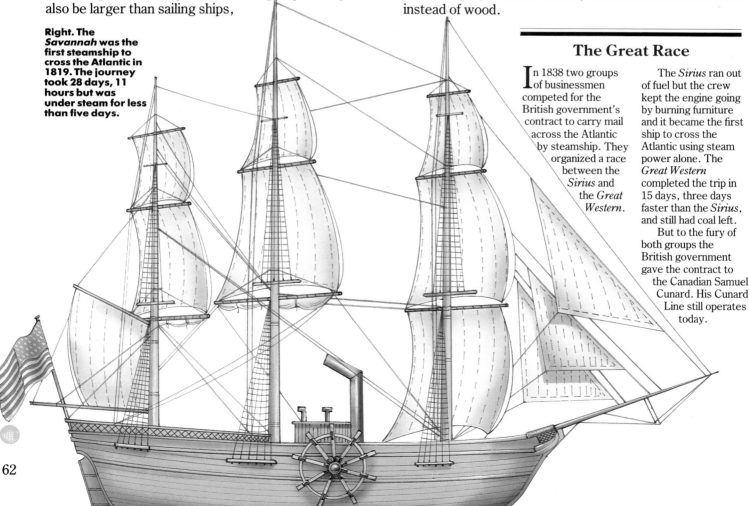

Right. The *Savannah* was the first steamship to cross the Atlantic in 1819. The journey took 28 days, 11 hours but was under steam for less than five days.

THE GREAT DAYS OF STEAM Exporting grain and meat from North America, or wool from Australia and New Zealand, together with emigrants traveling from Europe, all created fresh demands for shipping. Shipowners became prosperous.

In 1882 the *Dunedin*—the first refrigerated ship, carrying a cargo of meat and butter from New Zealand— arrived in London. Increasing supplies of food from abroad lowered prices in Europe, and British farming in particular suffered badly. At the same time, the European market for food encouraged farmers in North and South America, Australia and New Zealand to grow more.

Meanwhile, passenger travel by sea also increased. For the well-off, it became common to travel between America and Europe on business or holiday.

SHIPS OF WAR Navies were at first less keen than merchant shipowners to use steamships. As the early steamships burnt so much fuel, it would have been difficult in wartime to keep them at sea without having to return to port frequently for refuelling. Admirals also thought that iron hulls would be more easily damaged than wooden ones. But these were partly excuses for the fact that senior naval officers had been trained to use sailing ships and did not want to change their methods.

The French navy was the first to adopt steam power for its warships and gradually the advantages of steam

British dock workers were among the first to organize themselves to negotiate better pay and conditions. Here, London dockers vote for a strike in 1889.

and iron hulls came to be accepted by other countries. After about 1860 there was a great increase in building warships. These new ships had iron hulls and thick armor plate made of iron, and they were fitted with sails as well as steam engines. Revolving gun turrets were fitted to some battleships in the American Civil War (see pages 36–37) and these were so successful that other navies copied them. Later, steel armor plate up to 12 inches thick replaced the iron plate. Soon all the major world powers were rebuilding their navies.

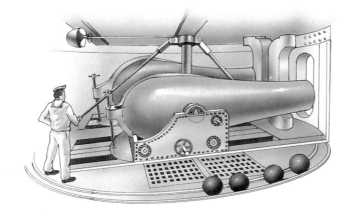

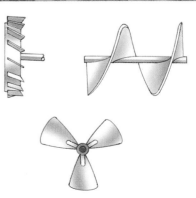

Above. The Federal steamer *Monitor* (right) rams the Confederate *Merrimac* in one of the first engagements between steam-powered warships.

Right. A canon and, far right, types of early propeller.

63

ADVANCES IN SCIENCE

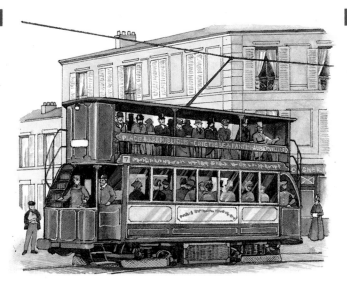

Above. The ability to generate electricity on a large scale was developed in the 1880s. This tram was operating in Paris by 1898.

Europeans and Americans in the nineteenth century were fascinated by science. They wanted to know more about the world than religious teaching told them. As the century went on, discovery after discovery seemed to provide new answers and opportunities. It seemed as if there was nothing that science could not do.

THE PATTERN OF DISCOVERY Nineteenth-century science followed a regular pattern. First, a scientist would work out a theory or idea about an aspect of science. Then others would try out the theory in experiments to see if it was correct.

In 1831 Michael Faraday (1791–1867) conducted experiments in Britain which demonstrated the laws of elctricity. His ideas were taken further by a Cambridge *physicist*, James Clerk Maxwell, who in 1873 proved the connection between electricity and magnetism. By 1880,

the German firm of Siemens had demonstrated the first electric train, making use of Maxwell's theories, and in 1881 the world's first two electric power stations opened in New York and London.

Michael Faraday provided the starting point for another important development. He found that the chemical *ether* numbed pain. At that time there was no way of putting someone to sleep before an operation; patients were fully conscious and had to be held down by strong men. In 1846 an American surgeon first used ether during an operation, but the next year a Scot called James Simpson (1811–1870) tried *chloroform*, which was easier to use. *Anaesthetics* allowed surgeons to carry out operations which had been impossible before.

SCIENCE IN THE UNIVERSITIES Science made great advances during the century in almost every area of human activity. There was a boom in scientific studies. Harvard University in the United States of America, and London, Cambridge, Glasgow, Paris and Berlin universities in Europe, became centers of scientific research. There was a growth in scientific societies, too. Some, like the Royal Society in Britain, funded expeditions and experiments. Others were more concerned to spread the new scientific knowledge more widely.

POPULAR SCIENCE Everyone could join in this new excitement. Science was not only for the scientists. In many cities, there were lectures and demonstrations which ordinary people could attend. For those who could not reach them, there were popular science magazines like *Chambers' Journal*, founded in Scotland in 1854, and *The Scientific American*.

Left. The first University to be founded in America was Harvard, at Cambridge, Massachusetts, which dates back to 1636. By 1840 it had become one of the great centers of learning in the US and was at the forefront of the scientific revolution.

1 2

People of Science

James Clerk Maxwell (1831–1879) was a Scottish physicist whose most important work was done at Cambridge University. His discovery of the link between electricity and magnetism was probably the most far-reaching of the nineteenth century. It led to the the use of electric motors, and all the electrical appliances we use today.

Louis Pasteur (1822–1895), a French chemist, devoted his life to investigating the causes and prevention of disease. One of his discoveries was that

James Clark Maxwell, who first linked electricity and magnetism in 1873.

bacteria in food could be killed by heating the food to 55°C. This process is still called "pasteurization."

Pasteur developed *vaccines* for use in the prevention of many diseases, including anthrax and rabies.

Below. An Italian scientist lectures on astronomy in London. Events like this were hugely popular and many people came to hear about the discoveries being made.

1 Science led to advances in the treatment of illness — and also in its prevention. Ideas about the causes of disease which were little more than superstition gave way to soundly-based scientific theories. In Britain, for example, Dr John Snow showed that an outbreak of cholera in London in 1854, which caused thousands of deaths, could be traced to the use of one infected street water pump. This led to a Public Health Act forcing all towns to provide clean water.

2 The invention of the telegraph — and later the telephone — had a dramatic impact on newspapers. In 1805 it took two weeks for news of the battle of Trafalgar to appear in *The Times*, in London. By 1851, the paper was able to print European news within hours. By 1866, news from North America could also be sent instantly by cable.

Above. A fanciful picture of students of the Scottish surgeon James Simpson, who first used chloroform as an anaesthetic. The rapid advance of science made many sceptical of its claims.

Newspapers gave an increasing amount of space to science, and more serious students could buy science encyclopedias in weekly parts and collect them to make a reference library.

GOING IT ALONE Not all the advances in science were made by trained scientists. Many people worked on their own on their ideas or inventions. One of these was the inventor of the telephone, Alexander Graham Bell (see page 69), who experimented in his spare time after his day's work as a professor of speech training. Another was Thomas Edison (see p. 61), who went to school for only a few months and taught himself all the science he knew. Some of his inventions are listed on page 61. Scientific knowledge was growing so fast that there were opportunities for everyone to take part.

THE DAWN OF THE OIL AGE

The American artist George Luks saw the oil companies as monsters aiming to devour the earth. He called this picture, dated 1899, *The Menace of the Hour*.

instead of coal in their engines. Between 1870 and 1900 the world's oil production multiplied 25 times.

Discoveries of oil brought prosperity to places which had never known it before, for example in parts of the Rocky Mountains in America. In 1901 oil was found in southern Texas and Louisiana, which until then had been among the poorest parts of the United States. Then other countries began to join in the oil boom: Mexico, Peru and, in the twentieth century, other South American countries and the Middle East.

The first oil well in the world was drilled at Oil Creek, Pennsylvania, in the United States of America in 1859. It was only 69 feet deep and produced just 25 barrels of oil a day.

UNWANTED RICHES Oil is a mixture of substances. At that time, people only used some of these. Most of the oil, including petroleum, was burned off or thrown away. What was left was *paraffin*, which was used mainly for oil lamps but also for cooking and heating. People had previously used vegetable or animal oil, particularly whale oil, for these purposes. Coal was the fuel in demand for industry and for use at home.

The oil industry grew very slowly in its early years, but there was a sudden change in the 1880s and 1890s, when gasoline and diesel engines were invented. By 1901 there were about 15,000 cars in use in the USA and almost as many in Europe. At about the same time the world's merchant and naval ships began to burn oil

THE OIL COMPANIES Prospecting for oil, and then sinking wells to bring it to the surface, is a long and costly business. In 1884, for example, foreign companies were allowed to prospect for oil in Mexico, but it was 16 years before any was found. Even after oil has been discovered, most of the cost of labor and materials must be spent before a single drop of oil is produced. Only large companies can afford these costs. The result was that from the start the oil industry was dominated by large companies such as Standard Oil in the USA, founded in 1870, and the Royal Dutch Company in Europe, formed in 1890. They were able to control production and prices, making huge profits. For a time in the 1880s Standard Oil controlled almost all the oil produced in the United States, about four-fifths of the world's production.

SHAPING NATIONS The full effect of oil on the world did not appear until the twentieth century, but the first signs of change began to be seen at the end of the 1800s. The USA produced by far the most of the world's oil and

A production field in the early days of the oil industry. In those days, the oil was stored in barrels, and it is still measured in barrels although they are no longer used.

The First Oil Billionaire

Right. A cartoonist's view of the "oil king" John D. Rockefeller (above).

HIS FAVORITE REMEDY. 1903

A man called six times to give Mr. Rockefeller a cure for dyspepsia. But John D. knows what he needs.

John Davison Rockefeller (1839–1937) left school at 14 to work as a clerk. Nine years later he became a partner in a small refinery. He found that the industry was badly organized. In 1870 he founded the Standard Oil Company, which soon took over almost all its rivals.

When Rockefeller retired in 1911 he was the richest man in the US. He gave over US $500,000,000 to educational projects, health care and medical research.

The power of oil: this graph shows the growth of US oil production from 1860 to 1900. As new uses were found for oil and people realized the potential profits which could be made, the development of oil production proceeded at an astonishing rate, setting the stage for the power oil would wield in the twentieth century.

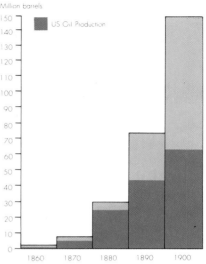

World Oil Production

Million barrels

US Oil Production

1860 1870 1880 1890 1900

Left. Oil lamps were decorative as well as practical. Until the gasoline engine was invented, lighting was the main use of oil.

this gave the country more industrial power. Western Europe did not produce any oil; it all had to be imported, which made it more expensive than it was in America. Many other parts of the world also depended on American oil supplies. Meanwhile, as people changed to oil, lower demand for coal led to the closure of many small mines.

THE COMMUNICATIONS REVOLUTION

The last half of the nineteenth century saw the start of the next revolution in world history—the communications revolution.

In 1800 the only way for most people to communicate over a distance was by letter, which was carried by horse and took several days to arrive. Ships signaled to each other with flags. Armies used *semaphore*, a message system involving either flags or signal arms in different positions.

MESSAGES BY WIRE These primitive methods of communication had been sufficient for a long time, but with the growth of industry and trade something better was needed now. In 1836 an American called Samuel Morse (1791–1872) came up with the first answer—the telegraph. At about the same time, two British scientists called Charles Wheatstone and William Cooke had a similar idea.

Morse's telegraph used electricity and magnetism to send messages in a code of dots and dashes along a wire. The first line to carry telegraph messages was opened between Baltimore and Washington, DC in 1845. Telegraphy made communication almost

A New York street festooned with wires in the early days of the telephone. Later, cables were laid underground in cities.

instantaneous, and it was very successful. Telegraph lines quickly spread between the main cities of North America and Europe, and by 1900 across other continents too. Britain and the rest of Europe were linked by underwater telegraph cable in 1851 and by 1865 there was a cable beneath the Atlantic Ocean.

THE TELEPHONE From the telegraph, it was only a step to sending voice messages, rather than coded ones, along a wire. There were many rivals to be the first to do this, but Alexander Graham Bell won the race in 1876. His first telephone was crude and difficult to hear, but improvements soon followed.

By 1878 the town of New Haven, Connecticut had the world's first telephone exchange (with 21 customers) and by 1879 there were

Before dialing was introduced, every telephone call had to be connected by hand by the operators. Consumers often had to wait for a line to be free, and calls took longer to connect.

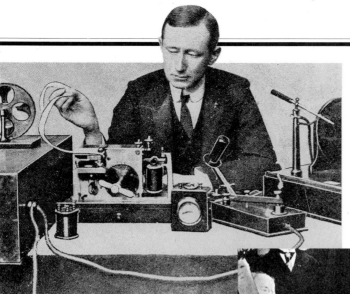

Left. The early days of radio. Reactions to Marconi's radio transmissions were cool until he used radio to report on the America's Cup yacht race in 1899. Below. Alexander Graham Bell, inventor of the telephone, opens up a new line from New York to Chicago, 1892.

Above. The British "Penny Black," 1840, was the world's first postage stamp.

Above. The ten cent stamp was one of the first in the USA.

1 Postal communication also made great strides in the 19th century, helped by railways and steam shipping. Britain introduced cheap postage in 1840 and the example was rapidly copied. In 1863 an international agreement was made to co-ordinate the post between different countries.

2 The cinema was developing during the last part of the 19th century. The first clear pictures were shown in the US by Woodville Latham and in England by Robert Paul, both in 1855. Thomas Edison built the first studio in 1893.

The Great Telephone Race

Three men were involved in the race to invent the telephone, which promised a great deal of money to the successful inventor. Alexander Graham Bell (1847–1922) was a teacher of the deaf who was interested in the telephone as an aid for the deaf. Elisha Gray (1835–1901), a telegraph engineer, wanted to use telegraph wires to carry voice messages. Thomas Alva Edison (1847–1931) was working on the same idea in secret, financed by the Western Union Telegraph Company.

The three men's applications for a *patent* — the right to profit from an invention — arrived at almost the same time in February 1876. The patent was awarded to Bell, though the decision was disputed. He heard the news on his 29th birthday.

After a slow start, the telephone rapidly became accepted after improved and long-distance lines were developed.

telephone networks in Britain, France and Norway. The telephone had soon become an essential part of doing business, but people were slower to accept it in their homes, partly for fear that their conversations would be overheard! The invention of automatic dialing in 1889 by an American called Almon B. Strowger helped to overcome this worry.

NO WIRES The third important communications invention came at the end of the nineteenth century. Guglielmo Marconi (1874–1937) was an Italian scientist who was interested in wireless telegraphy—sending telegraphic messages through the air by radio waves. He moved to London because the Italian government would not back him. In 1896 he began experiments in Britain and a year later he succeeded in sending a radio message over a distance of 9 miles. In 1898 he set up a system so that *lightships* could communicate with the shore by radio.

The rest of the story of radio belongs to the twentieth century, but its development arose out of the way that nineteenth-century inventors were interested in the possibilities opened up by a greater understanding of electricity and magnetism. Marconi was a pioneer of the technology that has given most of the world its main source of information and entertainment today.

TELEPHONES IN THE US 1880-1900

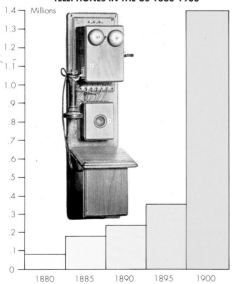

Millions (1.4, 1.3, 1.2, 1.1, 1.0, .9, .8, .7, .6, .5, .4, .3, .2, .1, 0) / 1880, 1885, 1890, 1895, 1900

MAKING SALES

The Industrial Revolution spread during the nineteenth century to factory production of almost everything anyone might need, from food to clothes and from toothbrushes to shoelaces. Manufacturers invested heavily in factory buildings and equipment. The way to get back the money they had spent was to make sure that customers bought *their* products and not those of a rival. At the same time, improved transport made it possible to distribute factory-made goods nationally and internationally.

BRAND NAMES Increasingly, manufacturers began to use *brand names* to identify their products, often with an easy-to-remember symbol or *trade mark*. One of the first people to see the value of giving products brand names and advertising them widely was William Lever (1851–1925), who started a soap business in Lancashire, England in 1884. Newspapers and magazines were not printed in color then, so Lever advertised mainly on brightly colored posters. The idea spread, and soon advertisements were urging people to buy

LIPTON'S ONE OF TEAS.

LIPTON'S TEA-GARDENS CEYLON

Tea Merchant. BY SPECIAL APPOINTMENT TO HER MAJESTY. THE QUEEN.

FINEST THE WORLD CAN PRODUCE 1/7 PER LB. NO HIGHER PRICE. RICH PURE & FRAGRANT 1/- and 1/4 PER LB.

LARGEST SALE IN THE WORLD

CHIEF OFFICES: CITY RD., LONDON. *Branches and Agencies throughout the World.*

Liptons made their reputation by promising good quality food at low prices. This was good news for people who had had to put up with inferior provisions.

The new department stores offered shoppers everything they needed under one roof.

particular brands of canned meat, ink, pen-nibs and other everyday products. The advertising industry had been born.

CHAIN AND DEPARTMENT STORES
An important change also happened in the shops. Shop-keepers realized that they could negotiate a better price from manufacturers—and so earn a greater profit for themselves—if they agreed to buy goods in large quantities. They then set up, or took over, several shops (a chain) to sell the goods.

One of the British pioneers of this style of shopkeeping was Thomas Lipton (1850–1931). By the 1880s he had a chain of grocery shops all over Britain and attracted customers to them by the clever use of advertising. Then he saw that he could make more money by owning his own tea and coffee plantations and running his own bacon and fruit-canning factories. His ideas were copied by many other grocers trying to attract customers. As wages began to rise towards the end of the century, people could afford to look for better quality goods as well as more varied and tastier food.

DRINK **Coca-Cola** At all Soda Founts and Carbonated in Bottles 5¢

THE IDEAL BEVERAGE FOR DISCRIMINATING PEOPLE

A GLASS ADDS TO THE PLEASURE OF A DRIVE OR A WALK BY BRIGHTENING AND REFRESHING THE FACULTIES.

IT IS A CHARMING—HEALTHFUL DRINK The MOST REFRESHING DRINK IN THE WORLD.

An early advertisement for Coca-Cola, originally promoted as a health drink.

ALL UNDER ONE ROOF
Another new type of shop was the department store. This was a large shop which supplied all kinds of goods, divided into separate departments, so that customers could do all their shopping under one roof. The first department store in Britain was Whiteley's in west London, which William Whiteley built up in the 1870s from a small drapery shop. Department stores aimed to make shopping entertaining by providing demonstrations of products, fashion shows and restaurants where musicians played while the customers had their meals. The idea was to make customers loyal to a particular store.

These developments were both good and bad for the customers. They led to better quality goods, because shopkeepers were afraid that disappointed customers might go to a rival. But they also made it harder for the customer to feel that he or she was getting the personal service that could be found in a smaller shop run by one individual. Many shops today are still trying to get this balance right.

The revolution in shopping.
Right. This New York drugstore has its merchandise set out invitingly on display. Shops began to look more as we know them today.
Below. Macy's department store in New York. Again, goods are arranged to catch the shopper's eye.

Shopping by Mail

Mail order was an important development in retailing towards the end of the nineteenth century. It reached its peak in the USA, where families in the newly settled west were out of reach of the city stores.

One of the most famous American mail order stores is Sears Roebuck, founded in Chicago in 1886 to sell watches by post. It soon extended its merchandise and by 1893 was publishing a 300-page catalog. This allowed families in remote areas to buy the latest goods and inventions.

Towards Today
TIME CHART

AD	EUROPE	NORTH AND SOUTH AMERICA	REST OF WORLD
1834			The Great Trek from Cape Colony begins
1839>1842			Britain launches First Opium War against China
1850>1864			Taiping Rebellion in China
1851	The Great Exhibition is held in London		Gold found in New South Wales and Victoria in Australia
1852	Cavour becomes prime minister of Piedmont		
1853			US warships sail into Tokyo Bay
1856			South African Boers establish the independent republics of Orange Free State and Transvaal
1856>1860			Britain and France attack China: the Second Opium War
1859	War between Piedmont and Austria		
1860	Rebellion in southern Italy		
1861>1871			The Maori Wars against the British
1865>1868			Civil war in Japan
1866	Prussia defeats Austria in the Seven Weeks' War		
1867		USA establishes a naval base at Midway Island in the Pacific USA buys Alaska from Russia	Diamonds discovered on the border of Orange Free State
1869		North America's first transcontinental railway opens	The Suez Canal opens
1870	Unification of Italy complete except for Vatican City Outbreak of the Franco-Prussian War	Standard Oil Company founded in the USA	
1871	France surrenders to Prussia. Wilhelm I proclaimed Kaiser of the German Empire		Delegation leaves Japan for America and Europe to study Western technology
1873	James Clerk Maxwell publishes his paper on electricity and magnetism		
1874		Barbed wire invented in the USA	
1876		The Centennial Exhibition is held in Philadelphia	
1879			Britain fights the Zulu War
1880	In Germany, Siemens demonstrates the first electric train		
1882	First refrigerated cargo ship arrives in Britain from New Zealand		
1884			Gold discovered in the Transvaal
1884>1885			War between China and France, ending in Chinese defeat
1885	European powers agree on "spheres of influence" in Africa		
1886		The Statue of Liberty completed in New York Harbor	
1888		Slavery abolished in Brazil	
1894>1895			War between China and Japan, ending in Chinese defeat
1896	Marconi begins experiments with radio		
1898			The Spanish-American War
1899			Britain declares war on the Boers
1899>1900			The Boxer Rising in China

GLOSSARY

anaesthetic A drug that stops a patient feeling pain, either locally (in a particular part of the body) or generally (unconsciousness).

assegai A light spear tipped with iron used for hand-to-hand fighting.

back-to-back A house which shares its back wall with another, so that there is no back door.

bankrupt A person who does not have enough money to pay his or her debts.

Boer South African of Dutch descent.

Buddhist A follower of the teachings of the Buddha.

caudillo A gang leader who controlled an area of South America.

censor To ban the publication of information or ideas.

chemical dye Dye made from synthetic rather than natural materials.

chloroform A general anaesthetic first used in 1847.

colony An area under the rule of another country.

democracy Government by the will of the majority of people.

discrimination Treatment of a group of people in a way that gives them inferior rights.

dynasty A ruling family that passes power on from one generation to the next.

emigrant A person who travels from one country to settle in another.

ether A general anaesthetic made by mixing acids with alcohol.

exile Prohibition from living in one's own country.

flail Whip-like implement used for threshing corn by hand.

heathen People with no religious beliefs.

Hindu(ism) Hinduism is a religion based on the Veda, its sacred book, which describes and explains the rituals which Hindus practice.

hunting and gathering The life-style of mankind in the earliest times, when people survived by hunting birds and animals and gathering wild fruits, nuts and berries.

immigrant A person who arrives in another country to settle there.

internal combustion engine An engine fueled by gasoline or diesel oil which produces energy by the burning of gases in closed cylinders.

Islam A religion which began in the Middle East and obeys the teachings of the prophet Mohammed.

Kaiser The emperor of Germany.

lightship A ship fitted with a powerful light which takes up a stationary position to warn other shipping of hazards.

loom A machine for weaving cloth.

mass-produced Identical goods made in large numbers.

mercenary A soldier who is paid to fight for a country other than his own.

Middle Ages A term used for the period of Western European history between the fifth and fifteenth centuries AD.

missionary A person who goes abroad to spread religious belief.

Muslim A follower of Islam.

mutiny An uprising of soldiers or sailors against their officers.

New World A term used for North, Central and South America after their discovery and development.

opium A narcotic drug made from the juice of opium poppy seeds.

pagan A worshipper of primitive gods.

pampas Grasslands of South America.

paraffin A fuel derived from oil and used for cooking, heating, diesel and aviation fuel. Also known as kerosene.

parliament The assembly which makes a country's laws. In the United Kingdom this consists of the non-elected House of Lords and the elected House of Commons.

patent The exclusive right to make, use or sell an invention.

petition A request for change made to those in authority and signed by a number of people.

phonograph An early record-player which used tinfoil cylinders instead of discs.

physicist A student of the nature of matter and energy.

Pilgrim Fathers The name given to the emigrants who sailed for America aboard the *Mayflower* in 1620 and founded the state of Massachusetts.

pioneer Name given to members of the families who moved westwards and began to develop the farmland of the American West.

plantation A farmstead of the southern United States which grew one main crop, such as cotton, and was worked by slave labor.

pollution Damage to the environment caused by human activity.

production line A factory system in which the manufacturing processes are arranged in sequence to maximize production and minimize time.

raw materials The basic items from which a manufactured product is made.

republican Believer in a system of government which has no monarch at its head.

samurai Japanese warriors.

secret ballot A system of voting using anonymous slips of paper.

semaphore A visual communications system using the position of flags to represent the letters of the alphabet.

tenement A building containing a number of homes on separate floors.

trademark A name or design adopted by a company to distinguish the goods it makes or sells.

trade union An organization of
workers aimed at improving pay and
conditions of work.

unification The bringing together
of a number of small states into one
country.

vaccine A substance injected into the
body to prevent disease.

INDEX

industrial injuries 12, 13
Industrial Revolution 9, 12–13, 16, 17, 20, 22, 27, 70
internal combustion engines 60
inventions 54, 60, 68–9
investment 17
Ireland 22–3, 56
iron and steel industries 14, 16, 54, 55, 60, 61
Islam 38
Italy 10, 11, 14, 20, 21, 27, 40, 42, 43, 51, 56, 72

Japan 44, 45, 46–7, 72
Jews 56–7
journalism 20, 21, 64–5
journals, scientific 64
jute 16

Korea 47
Kossuth, Louis 21

Lagos (Nigeria) 27
Latham, Woodville 69
Lee, Robert E. 36–7
Lever, William 70
Liberia 51
lightships 69
Lilienthal, Otto 59
limited liability companies 17
Lincoln, Abraham 36, 37, 40
linoleum 59
linotype 61
Lipton, Thomas 70, 71
Lister, Joseph 59
literature 19, 21
Livingstone, David 50
London 23
Lopez, Francisco 59
Luks, George 66

machinery
    factory 12–13
    farming 22, 23
    printing 38, 39, 60, 61
magnetism 64, 65
mail order shopping 71
Malta 27
Manchu dynasty 44, 45
manufacturing industries 9, 12, 13, 16, 60, 70

Maori Wars 53, 72
Maoris 53
maps
    American Civil War 37
    Austrian Empire (1848) 11
    British India (1805) 29
    Burke and Wills expedition 52
    China under foreign control 45
    colonial possessions in Africa (1870) 51
    colonization of New Zealand 53
    Europe (1915) 9
    European empires (1870) 27
    farming and industry in the USA 37
    growth of railways (1840–1870) 15
    Indian Mutiny 29
    industry in Europe (c.1850) 12
    Japanese expansion (1875–1900) 46
    Louisiana purchase 32
    revolutions (1830–1848) 10
    routes across America 32
    Russian Empire in Asia 24
    sea trading routes 17
    South Africa (1800–1900) 48
    South American states (1888) 59
    spread of cholera (1831) 19
    Suez Canal 51
    Trans-Siberian Railway 25
    unification of Germany 43
    unification of Italy 43
    Union and Confederate states 36
    US cattle trails 54
    US overseas interests (c.1900) 55
    US population density (1890) 57
    voyage of the *Beagle* 39
Marconi, Guglielmo 69, 72
Marx, Karl 11, 20, 21
mass production 60, 70
Mauritius 27
Mazzini, Giuseppe 21

medicine 59, 64
Melbourne 52
mercenaries 45
Mergenthaler, Otto 61
Mexico 27, 29, 66
Mill, John Stuart 21
missionaries 44, 51
monarchies 39
Morse, Samuel 68
Muslims 28

Napoleon 10, 11, 32
Napoleonic Wars 9, 10, 16, 40
Natal 49
naval bases, US 55, 72
navies 63
Netherlands 19, 26, 28, 34, 48
New South Wales 52, 72
New Zealand 24, 26, 27, 30, 40, 52, 53
newspapers 15, 20, 21, 38, 39, 65
Nicholas I, Tsar 25, 40
Nightingale, Florence 25
Norway 69
nursing 25

O'Connor, Feargus 21
oil companies 66
oil industry 66–7
oil lamps 67
oil wells 66
On Liberty 21
Opium Wars 44, 72
Orange Free State 49, 72
Origin of Species 39, 40

paddle-steamers 62
Paine, Tom 21
pampas 58, 59
Panama Canal 55
paraffin 66
Paraguay 59
Paris 11, 23, 43
passenger travel 14, 63
Pasteur, Louis 65
pasteurization 65
patents 69
Paul I, Tsar 24
Paul, Robert 69
Pearce, Samuel 38

Perkin, William 59
Peru 66
"Peterloo Massacre" 20
Philippines 55
phonographs 60, 61
photography 60, 61
physics 64, 65
Piedmont 42, 72
Pilgrim Fathers 36
pioneers 32–3
Pittsburgh 55
plantations 34
Poland 19, 40
political protest 20–1
pollution, industrial 18–19
population growth 10, 18, 23
population shift 22, 23
Portugal 26, 27, 28, 34, 40, 58
postage stamps 69
postal communications 15, 62, 69
potato famines 22–3, 30
poverty 10, 31, 39
printing 38, 39, 60, 61
production lines 60
Prussia 9, 42, 43, 72
public health 18, 19, 65
Puerto Rico 27, 40, 55

radio 69, 72
railways 14–15, 25, 31, 40, 41, 47, 72
raw materials 16, 27
refrigerated ships 53, 63, 72
republican government 21
Rights of Man, The 21
revolutions 9, 10, 11, 40, 42
Rockefeller, John D. 67
Rocket 15
rubber 59
Russia 9, 11, 14, 19, 20, 24–5, 44, 45, 47, 56
Russo-Japanese War 47

samurai 46
science 39, 59, 64–5
scientific societies 64
Sears Roebuck 71
secret ballots 21
semaphore 68
serfdom 24, 25
Seven Weeks' War 72

Further Reading

GENERAL REFERENCE
The Times Atlas of World History ed. by Geoffrey Barraclough (Hammond, 1989)

A History of Technology: The Late Nineteenth Century ed. by Charles Singer (Oxford, 1958)

The First Industrial Revolution by Phyllis Deane (Cambridge, 1980)

EUROPE
Europe Rules the World by Trevor Cairns (Cambridge, 1981)

Europe in the Nineteenth Century by Agatha Ramm (Longman, 1984)

Bismarck by Martin Booth (Greenhaven, 1980)

THE UNITED STATES
A Concise History of the American Republic by Samuel E. Morison, Henry S. Commager, and William E. Leuchtenburg (Oxford, 1983)

A Pocket History of the United States by Allan Nevins (Pocket Books, 1991)

The Story of America ed. by Elizabeth L. Newhouse (National Geographic Society, 1984)

THE REST OF THE WORLD
History of Southern Africa by Kevin Shillington (Longman, 1988)

Japan's Modernization by Edmund O'Connor (Greenhaven, 1980)

Picture Acknowledgement

The author and publishers would like to acknowledge, with thanks,
the following photographic sources:

p. 10 Photographie Bulloz; p. 11 Communist Party Archive; p. 13 (left) Berlin National Gallery,
(right) Hulton-Deutsch Collection; p. 14 Mansell Collection; p. 16 Western Americana Picture
Library; p. 17 (upper) Bridgeman Art Library, (lower) Hulton-Deutsch Collection; p. 19 (upper
left) Mansell Collection, (upper right) RIBA, (lower left) Bridgeman Art Library, (lower right)
Mansell Collection; p. 20 Fotomas Index; p. 21 (upper) AKG, (centre left and right) Hulton-
Deutsch Collection, (lower) AKG, p. 22 Mansell Collection; p. 23 Museum of English Rural Life;
p. 24 AKG; p. 25 (upper) Hulton-Deutsch Collection, (centre) John Massey-Stewart, (lower)
Wellcome Institute Library; p. 26 Visual Arts Library; p. 27 (centre) Ancient Art & Architecture
Collection, (right) Michael Holford; p. 28 (upper left) The 1st Queen's Dragoon Guards, (upper
right) Punch, (lower) Bridgeman Art Library; p. 31 (upper) Mansell Collection, (lower) New York
Historical Society; p. 34 Wedgwood Museum; p. 35 (upper and lower left) Hulton-Deutsch
Collection, (upper and lower right) Mary Evans Picture Library; p. 36 (centre) Western
American Picture Library, (right) Hulton-Deutsch Collection; p. 37 (upper and lower) Western
Americana Picture Library; p. 39 (left) National Portrait Gallery, (right) AKG; p. 39 (lower left)
Bridgeman Art Library, (centre) Robert Harding Picture Library; p. 42 AKG; p. 43 (left)
Hulton-Deutsch Collection, (right) AKG; p. 44 Wayland Picture Library; p. 47 (left) Fotomas
Index, (right) Bridgeman Art Library; p. 49 Mary Evans Picture Library p. 50 (left and centre)
Hulton-Deutsch Collection, (right) Mary Evans Picture Library; p. 52 Ancient Art & Architecture
Collection; p. 53 (left) State Library of Victoria, (right) Hocken Library, University of Otago;
p. 55 National Museum of the American Indian; p. 56 (upper) Bettmann Archive, (centre)
Hulton-Deutsch Collection; p. 57 Bettmann Archive; p. 58 Ann Ronan; p. 59 (upper) Mary Evans
Picture Library, (lower) Mansell Collection; p. 61 (upper) Mary Evans Picture Library, (lower)
ET Archive; p. 62 Western Americana Picture Library; p. 63 (upper) Mary Evans Picture
Library, (centre) Hulton-Deutsch Collection, p. 65 (upper and centre left, right) Mary Evans
Picture Library, London Planetarium, (lower left) Wellcome Institute Library; p. 66 Western
Americana Picture Library; p. 67 (left) Hulton-Deutsch Collection, (centre) Western Americana
Picture Library Rockefeller; p. 69 (upper) Mary Evans Picture Library, (centre) AT&T; p. 70
Hulton Picture Library; p. 71 (upper) Advertising Archive, (lower) Battmann Archive. Wherever
possible the copyright holder has been notified but we apologise if any material appears in error.